Hiking
Maine

by
Tom Seymour

(Formerly *The Hiker's Guide to Maine*)

FALCON™

Falcon Press® Publishing Co., Inc.,
Helena, Montana

A FALCON GUIDE

Falcon Press is continually expanding its list of recreational guidebooks. All books include detailed descriptions, accurate maps, and all the information necessary for enjoyable trips. You can order extra copies of this book and get information and prices for other Falcon books by writing Falcon Press, P.O. Box 1718, Helena, MT 59624, or calling 1-800-582-2665. Also, please ask for a free copy of our current catalog.

 Text pages printed on recycled paper.

CAUTION

Outdoor recreation activities are by their very nature potentially hazardous. All participants in such activities must assume the responsibility for their own actions and safety. The information contained in this guidebook cannot replace sound judgment and good decision-making skills, which help reduce risk exposure, nor does the scope of this book allow for disclosure of all the potential hazards and risks involved in such activities.

Learn as much as possible about the outdoor recreation activities you participate in, prepare for the unexpected, and be safe and cautious. The reward will be a safer and more enjoyable experience.

TABLE OF CONTENTS

ACKNOWLEDGMENTS

I owe a debt of gratitude to the following people for doing everything from acting as photographic subjects to providing information, from accompanying me on hikes to transferring material from one word processing program to another, and from suggesting hikes and helping make maps to providing moral support—even taking care of my house and dog while I was out hiking.

Special thanks to Ken Allen, Joe Arnette, John and Eleanor Avener, Pat Bailey, the Belfast & Moosehead Lake Railroad, Bill Drinkwater, Carolee Ferris, Lee Griffin, Tim Hall, Rick Henion, Alix Hopkins, Norm Jolliffe, Judy Kaiser, Peter MacPherson, Leo Mills, Jennifer Pierce, Vernon Shaw, Graham Taylor, and Dan Woodrow.

Precipice Trail in Acadia National Park. *Photo by Will Harmon.*

LOCATIONS OF HIKES

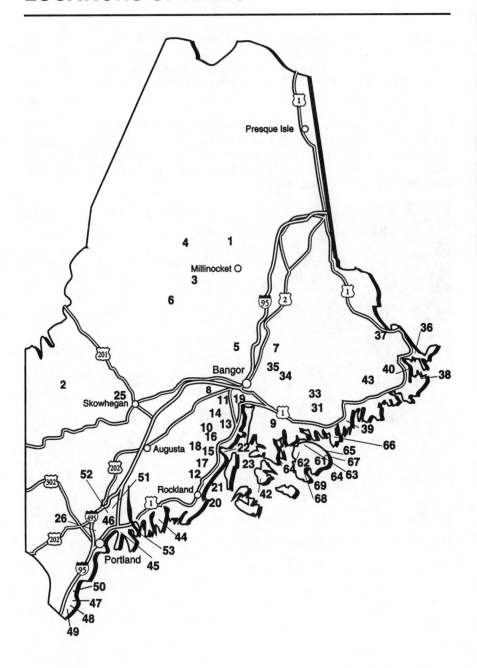

LEGEND

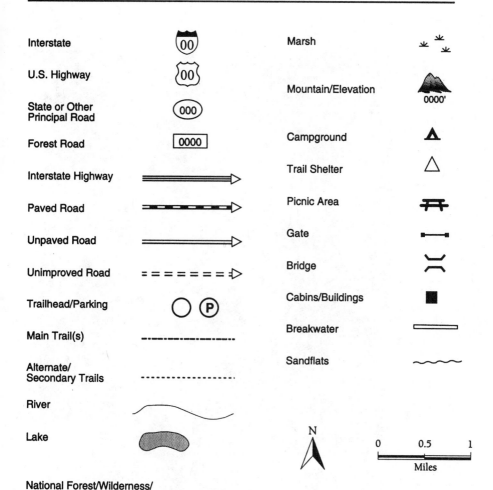

Interstate		Marsh	
U.S. Highway			
State or Other Principal Road		Mountain/Elevation	0000'
Forest Road	0000	Campground	
Interstate Highway		Trail Shelter	
Paved Road		Picnic Area	
Unpaved Road		Gate	
Unimproved Road		Bridge	
Trailhead/Parking		Cabins/Buildings	
Main Trail(s)		Breakwater	
Alternate/ Secondary Trails		Sandflats	
River			
Lake			
National Forest/Wilderness/ State Park Boundary			

N

0   0.5   1
Miles

Informational sign at Lake St. George State Park, Liberty, ME.

INTRODUCTION

Maine is a state of contrasts. From the potato fields of Aroostook County in the north to the pounding surf of Acadia and Mount Desert Island in the east, Maine contains a representative sampling of what nature, in its diversity, has to offer.

Although Maine is steadily growing, the entire population of the state is still less than that of a medium-sized city elsewhere. In fact, most of our cities are only cities by Maine standards. The city of Eastport has a population of around 2,000 individuals; the city of Belfast, a jumping-off point for visitors to the Downeast area, has a whopping population of 6,300. The bulk of our population lives in southern Maine. Even so, this section of the state offers startling beauty and one-of-a-kind hikes through salt marshes, pristine seashores, as well as an actual desert. Even Portland, Maine's largest city, is only minutes away from undisturbed countryside. About 90 percent of Maine is forested. Cities, roads, towns, lakes, rivers, and farms make up the remaining 10 percent. No wonder Maine chose to use "Vacationland" as the legend on its vehicle license plates.

In Maine, the past is closely interwoven with the present. Place names in Native American languages abound. Maine rivers, lakes, and streams are known by such tongue-twisters as Passagasswakeag, Sysladobsis, and Mooselookmeguntic. Maine towns are steeped in history. The village of Castine has been held by the French, Dutch, British, and lastly, we Americans. The first American naval defeat happened at Castine, nearly resulting in a personal disaster for no less a personage than Paul Revere.

Maine has its share of public land in the form of state parks and Acadia National Park, known as the "crown jewel," but the bulk of wild Maine is privately owned. Lovers of the outdoors here owe much to the generosity of private landowners, whether they be large paper companies or individuals. This being the case, it is even more important in this time of lessening access to respect landowners who allow it. As you hike across private land on some of the trails in this book, leave everything as you found it. Carry out whatever you carry in. Go the extra mile and take out litter left by those who came before you. Only by showing care and respect will we help this unique tradition of unlimited public access continue.

What Is a Hike?

For the purposes of this guidebook, a hike can be described in various ways: a difficult trek to the peak of a mountain, a leisurely stroll along a windswept seashore, a walk around an island on Penobscot Bay, a journey through a town or city with stops of historical interest. Hiking is getting out and traveling by your own means, with or without a particular destination. This last point needs to be stressed. Just because a hike listed in this book has a specific beginning and end doesn't mean that a hiker must reach the

1

Clintonia, a common woodland flower blooms in June.

end of the trail. The benefits of hiking are in the doing—nothing else takes precedence.

People of all ages and physical conditions can go for hikes. Obviously, you need to be in top physical shape for mountain climbing, a strenuous activity, but hiking is not just climbing peaks. Many trails listed in this book are wheelchair-accessible, while other hikes are ideally suited for groups, families with young children, or people who are physically challenged in one way or another. After all, hiking is a state of mind, not a strict physical regimen.

Hiking with children can be a learning experience. Children are observant; what may seem common or familiar to you will be new and exciting when seen through the eyes of a child. It is worth your time to take children on hikes in areas that provide educational opportunities. Some places have guided tours and discussions on plant and animal life as well as history. These are of immeasurable value to youngsters.

My grandfather took me on hikes through the local woods, taking time to identify plants and animal signs, giving me valuable hands-on experience. Because of his inspiration, my future as a lover of the outdoors was solidly entrenched. The sights, sounds, and smells that I encountered on my hikes with him are with me forever. You can give similar memories to other youngsters.

Wildlife

An old Maine saying contends that there is nothing in the Maine woods that will harm a person. This is essentially true, but an attitude of respect is still the best policy regarding Maine wildlife. Maine is said to have the largest black bear population in the continental United States, so the possibility of a bear confrontation can never be ruled out.

Although most bears are eager to leave an area once they detect your scent or see you, a sow with cubs can feel threatened—and so threaten you. Leaving foodstuffs on the ground or uncovered in a tent is one way to invite a visit from a bear. Hiking with dogs also can increase bear hazards. Unlike grizzlies out West, black bears can climb trees, so in the event of a situation, stay on the ground. If you see a bear, the best policy is to slowly back away from the area. Do not run, since this may excite the animal. One final resort in a bear confrontation is to wave your hands and yell at the bear. If this fails, many lives have been saved simply by striking the bear on the nose with whatever object is handy. Treat bears with respect and they will not bother you.

Maine also has a large moose population, so the possibility of seeing a moose is as great or greater than that of seeing a bear. A Maine moose may be four to five times larger than a black bear. This, coupled with typical moose unpredictability, means that all moose should be treated with caution. A cow moose with young is always dangerous, and a bull moose

In summer, moose take to ponds to escape biting insects and to eat aquatic vegetation.

in the autumn rut can be belligerent. Enjoy these giant members of the deer family from a safe distance and never underestimate them.

Maine is home to a new predator, the eastern coyote, also known as the brush wolf. These animals are the result of mating between a subspecies of Canadian timber wolf and the coyote of the northern plains. While some western coyotes are not much larger than a red fox, these eastern coyotes have been known to reach a weight of 70 pounds. Few documented attacks by eastern coyotes exist in Maine, and these were by young animals, probably more interested in playing than doing bodily harm. Still, the size and nature of these beautiful animals dictate that they be treated with respect. Coyotes usually will not bother you, except if you are a light sleeper. Their howling is now a regular nighttime sound in Maine.

Although their presence is not officially recognized, the number of mountain lion sightings in Maine continue to multiply. From mountain regions to suburban backyards, Mainers are reporting seeing big yellow cats with long tails. In fact, sightings are so common that they are no longer news. In order for the Maine mountain lion to be officially recognized, their existence needs to be documented. Scat, hair samples, and plaster casts of tracks will go a long way toward proving, once and for all, that the mountain lion is back to stay. A picture of a Maine mountain lion against a specific, identifiable background would be particularly helpful. Bring a camera.

Southern New England presently is experiencing a rabies problem. This outbreak is expected to reach Maine in the near future. Raccoons, skunks, and foxes are all suspect. If, when hiking in Maine, you encounter an animal that seems unafraid, leave the area quickly and report the sighting to a Maine game warden or state trooper.

Thankfully, Maine has no poisonous snakes. Those people used to watching the ground ahead of them for snakes can relax in the Maine woods. Insects, though, present a different problem.

Insects and Their Kin

As spring awakens the Maine coast, and daytime temperatures climb into the 60s, insects become a problem. Black flies, fierce biting gnats, are perennial nuisances in Maine. Black flies are mostly a springtime problem in southern and central Maine, but some northern areas are pestered by them all summer. The flies attack all exposed areas of the body. They also have the habit of crawling up pant legs and inside stocking tops. These insects inject the skin with a local anesthetic before biting, so you are often unaware that you are being bitten. Treat all exposed areas with insect repellent containing 100 percent Deet, diethyl toluamide. Wear long-sleeved shirts and fasten pant legs to boot tops with an elastic band. Wearing shorts, sneakers, and a tee shirt in black fly season will result in dozens of agonizing bites. During extremely dense outbreaks, a head net is invaluable. Carry one in your pack.

Mosquitoes are prevalent in Maine mostly during the wet seasons of late spring and early summer. Use the same precautions that you would for black flies.

No-see-ums, small biting midges, are summertime nuisances in many parts of Maine. These minute insects descend upon people in clouds, usually from sundown until the wee hours of the morning. Although no-see-um bites are not long lasting, the burning sensation resulting from dozens of bites is quite uncomfortable. No-see-ums are kept at bay by insect repellent or a combination of repellent and fine netting.

Lyme disease has crept into Maine in recent years. Interestingly, while long pants and long sleeves are helpful in warding off black fly and mosquito attacks, they provide hiding places for the ticks that carry the bacteria that cause this disease. Because of this, you need to check the seams of your clothing for ticks. The best way to avoid ticks is to avoid touching trailside brush. Stay on the trails and treat your clothing with insect repellent to greatly reduce danger from ticks.

Weather

Maine weather is never predictable. Sea fogs, cold fronts from Canada, and warm fronts from the south combine regularly to create a wide variety of weather conditions. Summertime temperatures can stay in the high 90s

Town of Bar Harbor—seen from summit of Cadillac Mountain.

for days, and winter temperatures can see readings of 40 degrees Fahrenheit below zero. An average summer temperature in Maine, if you can call anything about our weather average, is between 70 and 80 degrees. But then the temperature on the Fourth of July might be in the high 30s, and in the 50s on Christmas Day.

You can't anticipate what the weather will be, so come prepared. Even in summer, nights are often cool enough for a sweater. The last frost in Maine can be as late as June, and the first frost may come as early as August. Warm spells can stay with the Pine Tree State from summer through fall. The old Maine saying, "If you don't like the weather, just wait a minute," is based on fact, so believe it.

Autumn is a time of fabulous beauty in Maine, but it is also hunting season. October and November are the months when Mainers go afield for sport and to put meat on the table. When hiking wooded areas of Maine in the fall, wear an orange hat or vest.

Although Maine winters can be severe, hiking is not relegated to the warm months. Coastal areas do not get as much snowfall as inland areas, so, while it may be chilly, a brisk hike along the seashore can be exhilarating. Do remember that skim ice can form on seaside rocks, making for slippery going. Also, never walk on rocks that are covered with seaweed, since they are slippery no matter what the season. Some hiking trails are also used as snowshoeing and cross-country ski trails. This is another good way to see the country.

Firearms

Hikers in other states sometimes carry handguns with them for protection against human predators. In Maine, you need not carry a firearm when hiking anywhere in the state. In fact, carrying a gun without a hunting license or special permit may be a crime in certain instances. Many rural Mainers never lock the door to their homes or their cars and often find it amusing when a tourist locks his or her car only to shop at the corner grocery for a few minutes. By and large, Maine is a friendly state, so relax and enjoy it. Maine advertises itself with the slogan, "Maine, The Way Life Should Be."

Water

Although Maine is blessed with an abundance of streams, ponds, rivers, and lakes, no water can ever be considered safe to drink. Giardia may be present, as well as fecal matter from an upstream source. Some springs are marked as safe for drinking. These you can draw water from and use without fear, but as a rule, you should purify all water by boiling for a few minutes or by adding purification tablets.

Campfires and Fire Danger

Most state parks in Maine provide fire pits. No special permit is needed to build a campfire in these areas. But in areas other than state parks, fire

Immature ostrich ferns (fiddleheads) are a favorite wild food in Maine.

The low-growing bunchberry is a member of the dogwood family.

builders must have written permission from the landowner and must also notify the local fire warden of their intent to kindle a fire.

Typically, winter, spring, and early summer are not particularly dangerous times for fires in Maine, but late summer and fall are prime times. Often the commissioner of Inland Fisheries and Wildlife will close the woods because of a high level of fire danger. You can get updates on the level of fire danger from any Forest Service official and also from the National Oceanic and Aeronautic Administration (NOAA) radio station. I suggest you purchase a portable weather radio to help in planning your hikes. These crystal-controlled radios are no larger than a pack of cigarettes, and with them weather information is available 24 hours a day. For slight cost, these are one of the best investments you can make.

Miscellaneous Notes

Most of the hikes in this book can be done in a day. Several hikes are quite new, on private land only recently opened to the public or on trails that are only now being established. The hikes included in this book should show you a bit of the real Maine, surpassing its Hollywoodized image. Mountains, seashores, ponds, salt marshes are all described here.

Do not forget that while Maine is noted for its unbeatable scenery and clean, pine-scented air, people are Maine's most valuable resource. Do not be surprised when a motorist waves to you as you walk down a country road. Wave back. You may meet that individual later; by waving, you will have initiated a friendship that could last for years to come. Enjoy Maine's friendly and non-assuming people as well as the state's seashores and woods.

As mentioned earlier, when hiking during the black fly season, long sleeves and long pants are important. Many seaside hikes will be insect-free, and you will need no more than shorts, a lightweight shirt, a hat with a visor to keep the sun from your eyes, and a good supply of sunscreen. Never forget to smear exposed skin with sun block. Even cloudy days can be dangerous—perhaps more dangerous than clear days, since the dangerous rays are still there, whether you know it or not.

A list of things to bring on longer hikes can be found in the Appendix to this book. While hiking even for a few hours, however, you may find a backpack is useful to carry a notebook, lunch, canteen, binoculars, and camera. If you really want to go native, use a pack basket. These can be purchased at any outdoor store in Maine. These baskets are mostly made of ash or maple splints by local artisans. They are designed to distribute weight properly to reduce backaches, and come in a variety of sizes.

Finally, in addition to this book, you should obtain a copy of DeLorme Mapping Company's *The Maine Atlas and Gazetteer*. This book features seventy maps, detailing the entire state of Maine. The state map on the back cover features numbered grids, making it easy to find the pages you want without thumbing through the entire book. These maps will help put the area you plan to hike in perspective with the surrounding areas, and give you a better idea of just where you are in the state. Most bookstores and sporting good stores in Maine sell this book. You may also obtain one by writing to DeLorme Mapping Company, P.O. Box 298, Freeport, Maine 04032

WINTER HIKING

Peace, solitude, and the chance to study nature up close are some of the reasons hikers are drawn to the Maine woods in the winter. Winter hiking is growing more popular in the state. Often, coastal Maine and the offshore islands have only light snow cover, allowing you to hike without any special equipment other than a good pair of insulated boots. Even in wooded areas with deep snow, hikers with snowshoes and skiers are not thwarted by winter. However you go about it, hiking in wintertime can be a unique adventure.

Clothing

Winter hiking does have some caveats. Sudden temperature drops can cause a perspiring hiker to become chilled, inviting hypothermia.

Modern technology has given active people some wonderful outdoor gear. New synthetic clothing is durable, warm, and—best of all—lightweight. Many synthetics also "breathe" and are thus capable of expelling moisture rather than trapping it. For all that, traditional fabrics still have a place in the hiker's tote bag. Cotton is comfortable and lightweight. Wool is heavier than cotton or synthetics, but it is as tough as nails and allows you to retain body heat even when it is soaking wet. Synthetics and cotton are useless when wet. One of my favorite garments is a wool coat made in 1947, still intact, although the material around the buttonholes has frayed.

Whether you opt for clothing made of synthetic or natural fibers, you should wear layers of clothing rather than rely upon a heavy coat and single pair of warm pants. Layering permits you to regulate body heat with great efficiency. The moment you begin to perspire, you should stop and open up your outer jacket so that you do not become drenched with sweat, which is an invitation to hypothermia. If the weather turns warm, you can remove a layer or two of clothing and put it back on when the temperature drops.

My clothing for winter hiking consists of a set of cotton thermal underwear (top and bottom), lightweight wool pants, a cotton flannel shirt, a wool sweater, and a two-piece nylon outer jacket, consisting of an insulated inner jacket and a tightly woven windbreaker. If things begin to warm up on the trail, I simply remove the insulated inner jacket and put it in my pack basket or tie it around my waist. Later in the afternoon, I usually need to put the inner jacket back on. In late winter, when the temperature is at or above freezing, I omit the nylon outerwear in favor of a lightweight wool jacket worn over a sweater.

Bring enough clothing to keep warm, but wear only what you need to be comfortable, since overdressing will fatigue you and cause needless perspiration. Evening temperatures in Maine can vary wildly from daytime temperatures. Do not find yourself at the end of a long trail at sundown without proper attire. Common sense is the best guide here. Never expect temperatures to remain constant, and be prepared for sudden snow squalls as well as fog and rain. Properly dressed, you will be in no danger.

Snowshoeing

The art of snowshoeing is a way to enjoy the outdoors in spite of the season. Most sporting goods stores carry a variety of snowshoes, as do many outdoor catalogs. Most hikers opt for trail snowshoes, in a long and narrow style. These snowshoes are built for speed but are harder to maneuver in close quarters than shorter, rounder types. Long, thin snowshoes with upturned tips and a peg on the end are your best bet for winter hiking on established trails, while shorter and rounder types are preferred off trail.

Most Maine hikers make brief day trips when using snowshoes. Short daylight hours and subfreezing temperatures rule out extended hikes. Even if you are in robust health and fine physical condition, snowshoeing can be rigorous exercise. Given ever-changing snow conditions, a trip that takes an hour on bare ground may take twice as long on snowshoes. As the sun warms the top layer of snow, and the crust begins to melt, you may break

Winter hiking can be fun.

through with each step. Wet snow may stick to the webbing of your shoes, especially if you have the older style webbing, made of rawhide. Modern synthetic webbing is superior in this respect, since rawhide webbing tends to stretch when wet, while the synthetic stuff remains uniformly taut.

Breaking trail through deep snow is difficult work. Two or more snow hikers can switch off at regular intervals, eliminating undue fatigue for any one individual. One of the plusses of using snowshoes as opposed to cross-country skis is that with snowshoes your hands are free. You can walk along in a normal manner, without much thought as to what to do with your hands.

Wildlife

Wildlife can be active in winter. Although most songbirds have long since left for warmer regions, many intrepid species are year-round residents. Some birds you may expect to encounter during a winter walk in the Maine woods are red- and white-breasted nuthatches, black-capped and boreal chickadees, common crows, blue jays, pileated and hairy woodpeckers, and various owls, the most common being the great- horned owl. You may also see wild turkeys, ruffed grouse, and bald eagles. Two more rare birds found in northern Maine are the gray jay and the spruce grouse. Gray jays are notorious camp robbers, but their inquisitive personality has endeared them to generations of Maine woodsmen. Spruce grouse are protected in Maine because of their scarcity and vulnerability.

They are unafraid of people and often refuse to fly when confronted. A sighting of either of these birds is a treat.

A bonus for the winter hiker is the chance to see and identify a mind-boggling number of animal tracks. Mammals of all sizes leave proof of their passing in the snow. A walk in the woods just after a fresh snow may reveal the tiny prints of mice scurrying from one tunnel to the next. A few feet down the trail you may see where a snowshoe hare lost a race with a red fox. A small set of tracks leading to a tree can indicate the haphazard wanderings of a red squirrel. White-tailed deer, bobcats, lynx, and majestic moose all wander the Maine woods in the winter.

On warm days in late winter, snow fleas, or springtails, blanket the snow around the base of trees. What appears to be a layer of black soot is actually hundreds of thousands of minute insects, warmed to action by the rays of the sun.

Be aware that winter is a stressful time for all wildlife. Food is hard to come by, and low temperatures can quickly kill a weakened animal or one that is overheated from exhaustion. Do nothing to stress any animals or birds, since all their strength and energy must be used to survive. An animal forced to run away from a hiker may be forced to waste precious calories.

HIKING WITH CHILDREN

Hikers with young children often eschew outdoor activities until their kids are older. That's a shame, since Maine has a number of hiking trails that are carefully planned to provide just the kind of hikes that youngsters can appreciate. Many of these hikes are located in scenic natural areas with visitor centers featuring interpretive programs and guided tours.

Of course, any hike you take as a family will be a good one, as long as the children are not stressed beyond their limits. Hiking is the kind of outing that draws family members together. Sharing new vistas helps form spiritual bonds; whether those vistas take in the view from a cliff overlooking the Atlantic Ocean or open to the realization that even such seemingly insignificant life forms, such as the Tomah mayfly, the extra-striped snaketailed dragonfly, or several species of freshwater mussels, have suffered as a result of human incursion into their habitat and are candidates for the endangered species list.

Children have a natural desire to explore and learn about nature. Small children are particularly open to suggestion, so now is the time to impart a sense of responsibility toward our natural world. Hopefully, through your example, the children of today will be the low-impact, responsible hikers and campers of tomorrow.

What to Take With You

You will want to carry field guides to plants, animals, reptiles, insects, birds, and amphibians when hiking with children. As you hike, your children will be drawn to the vast numbers of life forms along the trail. Allow them to help you to identify an insect or flower. Such lessons learned in early life will not be forgotten.

Being prepared is of vast importance when hiking with children. A bee sting or bug bite can ruin the day for a child, while it may be only a mild inconvenience for an adult. Carry insect repellent as well as some kind of antiseptic that will ease the sting. One brand of insect repellent popular in Maine not only contains a small amount of Deet (the most effective ingredient in any insect repellent) but has pine tar as well. Pine tar has a distinct, refreshing odor that will help a child's mind recollect the Maine outdoors.

Being cold and wet on a hike will have a negative impact on your child that may well make her or him reluctant to go on future hikes. Bring plenty of warm clothes as well as rain gear. Do not forget sunscreen. A sunburn resulting from a hike will spoil the memory of the day.

Recommended Hikes

Many of the hikes in this book are suitable for families with young children, but some are especially suitable because they feature guided and self-guided tours as well as nature programs for the whole family. The following are highly recommended for families with children:

Wolfe's Neck State Park, Freeport.

The park encompasses more than 200 acres and has about 5 miles of hiking trails. Your child will be thrilled to see the ecosystems here, including mature white pine and hemlock forests, a salt marsh estuary, and the rugged shorelines of Casco Bay and the Harraseeket River. The park also features regularly scheduled nature programs, centering upon such themes as Children and Parents Together in Nature, Conservation for Kids, and Edge of the Sea, an introduction to the ecology and natural history of the shore. For more information on these programs, contact the Maine Bureau of Parks and Recreation, Department of Conservation, State House Station 22, Augusta, Maine 04333; (207) 289-3821.

The Game Farm and Visitors Center, Gray.

The Game Farm and Visitors Center began as the site of the state's pheasant-rearing program, but that was phased out in 1982. Now the Game Farm is used to care for orphaned and injured wildlife, and, as such, is home to many animals that for various reasons cannot be returned to the wild. In addition, the Game Farm offers a visitor center with educational displays, a garden of wildlife-attracting trees and shrubs, interpretive signs, trails, and a 2-acre wetlands and wildlife exhibit area. For further information, contact the Maine Department of Inland Fisheries and Wildlife, 284 State Street, Augusta, Maine 04333; (207) 657-4977.

The Wells National Estuarine Research Reserve.
The Wells Reserve is part of the national Estuarine Research Reserve System. It protects 1,600 acres of marshes, shorelines, estuary waters, and uplands. The Wells Reserve features guided tours through parts of a 7-mile trail system. Additionally, special tours are offered on wildflowers, birds, night skies, research, and the historic buildings of the old Laudholm Farm. Specially geared to children are the Discovery and Junior Researchers programs. The Discovery Program invites children and parents to explore the reserve with 10 "animal" tour guides. The Junior Researchers Program is a series of weekly sessions for children ages 9 through 11. For more information, contact Wells Reserve, Rural Route 2, Box 806, Wells, Maine 04090; (207) 646-1555.

The Rachel Carson National Wildlife Refuge.
The refuge offers a mile-long, self-guided interpretive trail, with songbirds, waterfowl, and shorebirds visible from the trail. Information and leaflets are available at refuge headquarters. The Rachel Carson trail hike can be combined with a trip to the nearby Wells National Estuarine Research Reserve. For further information write to the refuge manager at the Rachel Carson National Wildlife Refuge, Rural Route 2, Box 751, Route 9 East, Wells, Maine 04090; (207) 646-9226.

TRAILS FOR HIKERS WITH SPECIAL NEEDS

Federal, state, and private agencies in Maine recognize the need to provide access to the outdoors for people with special needs. No longer must hikers with disabilities be consigned to the sidelines, since Maine offers numerous opportunities for them to get outdoors.

Of notable interest is the town of Jackman, Maine. Not far from the Canadian border, Jackman proudly boasts of being one of the first (if not the first) barrier-free towns in the nation. Additionally, a local nonprofit organization there, Disabled Outdoor Experiences (DOE), is dedicated to providing outdoor sports and activities for the physically challenged. DOE hosts an annual wilderness rendezvous, featuring a variety of primitive and modern shooting events, tomahawk throwing, archery, and fishing trips from a pontoon boat. Plans for a nature center at Jackman are underway, with wheelchair-accessible trails through the woods and along the Moose River. For more information about Jackman and DOE, write to Disabled

The barrier-free Woodcock Trail.

Outdoor Experiences, P.O. Box 607, Jackman, Maine 04946, or call (207) 465-3064 on weekdays, (207) 668-4837 on weekends.

Some of the hikes listed later in the book have trails with access for those with disabilities. Some of these trails are as follows:

Wolfe's Neck Woods, Freeport.

Wolfe's Neck Woods features a half-mile-long accessible path, hardened with stone dust, which connects to packed gravel sidewalks and the interpretive area. These paths may be soft in early spring. For more information, contact the Bureau of Parks and Recreation, Maine Department of Conservation, State House Station 22, Augusta, Maine 04333; (207) 289-3821.

The Game Farm and Visitors Center, Gray.

The new wetlands and wildlife area at the Game Farm features a trail with access for those with disabilities. Contact the Maine Department of Inland Fisheries and Wildlife, 284 State Street, Augusta, ME 04333; (207) 657-4977 or TDD (207) 287-4471.

Wells National Estuarine Research Reserve.

The Laird-Norton Trail, between Barrier Beach Road and the Overlook, is a boardwalk, barrier-free and wheelchair-accessible. Contact the Wells Reserve, Rural Route 2, Box 806, Wells, Maine 04090; (207) 646-1555.

Rachel Carson National Wildlife Refuge.

The Upper Wells Division of the refuge offers a mile-long, barrier-free, self-guided interpretive trail. Contact the refuge manager at Rachel Carson National Wildlife Refuge, Rural Route 2, Box 751, Route 9 East, Wells, Maine 04090; (207) 646-9226.

Portland Trails

Portland Trails is a nonprofit organization with the goal of creating a 30-mile network of trails, pond loops, riverbank paths, bikeways, and shoreline walks linking all of the city of Portland's green spaces. The organization's newest endeavor is the development of the Eastern Promenade. This area consists of 30 acres of Casco Bay waterfront, with more than a mile of shoreline. The Eastern PromenadeTrail will be paved and barrier-free, allowing use by people in wheelchairs, and is expected to be completed sometime in 1996. For more information, contact Alix W. Hopkins, Executive Director, Portland Trails, P.O. Box 17501, Portland, Maine 04101; (207) 775-2411.

If you are a hiker with special needs or are assisting someone who is disabled, you will have to use your own judgment as to what constitutes an acceptable and accessible hike. Read the hike descriptions in this book and make your decisions accordingly. You will find many places to enjoy Maine's outdoor beauty. Unspoiled nature is there to comfort and renew us all.

HOW TO USE THIS GUIDE

This book can serve as a basic reference tool, a source of information about interesting places to visit in Maine. The hikes listed here are by no means the only worthwhile spots in the state, but they are a representative sample of what Maine has to offer.

The guide is set up to give you the information you need to anticipate what each hike will bring. Each hike entry includes the following:

General description.
This is simply a broad description of the hike and terrain it covers.

General location.
This tells you where the hike is located in larger Maine, often giving the closest town and county.

Maps.
For hikers who want more information than is given in this book, this lists additional maps available for the area of the hike.

Degree of difficulty.
This is by nature an arbitrary classification. What might be easy for one person may represent a challenge for another. In this book, "easy" means individuals in good health should have no difficulty on the trail. Some easy hikes listed here do have significant elevation gains, but nothing that cannot be taken in stride by a healthy person. "Moderate" means some exertion will be needed. If you are not feeling up to a bit of work, avoid these hikes. "Difficult" means just that. These hikes have steep elevation gains and rough terrain; they may be dangerous for an unfit hiker. Unless you are in excellent shape, avoid hikes listed in this way. A few hikes fall in between classifications and are labeled as such—"easy to moderate," for example. This classification means that the hike is generally easy but may have a few steep or rough areas.
The hike description will also give you clues about the hike's difficulty.

Length.
Hike lengths are given in total miles, generally round-trip distances. Many of these distances were taken from reading by a pedometer. Your personal readings may vary, since most individuals walk faster or slower than others and with different gaits and strides. Consider these distance measurements to be close, but not exact.

Elevations.
This listing gives the maximum elevation above sea level reached on the hike.

Water availability.
This note tells you whether or not there is potable water on the hike. You are advised to carry water on hikes where streams or taps are not available.

Special attractions.
Natural history information, historical facts and sites, landscape or seascape views, and pertinent attractions are listed in this section. If the hike is particularly good for families with children or physically challenged people, it is noted here.

Best season.
Since spring and fall come to different parts of Maine at different times, this section lists months of the year instead of the more general seasons. Use this information to help as you plan when to do hikes, especially in muddy areas. The first spring month given here takes into account the end of mud season; the last month listed tells you when it is safe to hike without encountering severe snowstorms.

For more information.
This listing gives addresses and phone numbers of agencies or individuals to contact for more details about this hike or region.

Finding the trailhead.
Many parts of Maine have few towns, cities, or even roads. This section tells you how to find the trailhead from the nearest large town or the most easily recognized reference points.

The hike.
The hike description is intended to acquaint you with the hike before you actually begin. Read this passage thoroughly to know what to look for as you walk or climb. You may, of course, take the book with you for reference as you go. Bear in mind that sections of trails change from time to time, so specifics in the hike description may no longer apply. Do not panic if a certain tree or flower is not where the description suggests it may be; just follow the trails and go by marked signs and immovable objects, as listed.

Use this book while planning hikes and as a companion on the trail. You may also want to read it fireside to help bring the stark beauty of Maine into your home anytime you open its pages.

THE HIKES

INLAND HIKES OVERVIEW

Inland Maine is wild and scenic country dotted with lakes, rivers, and ponds. And although mountains dot Maine's coast, none of them can match the remote splendor of the inland peaks.

The inland region is the last stronghold of the Eastern wilderness. Scenes akin to what Native Americans witnessed previous to the arrival of the first European settlers have remained nearly unchanged in such places as Baxter State Park. The great northeast can be experienced at its best in Maine's interior. As stewards of this northwoods wonderland, we must do our part to insure that the wilderness will be here years after we are gone. Low-impact and no-impact hiking and camping are mandatory if we are to preserve our wild regions.

Hikers who travel to some of Maine's inland valleys will experience the lowest temperatures in the state—often the lowest temperatures in the nation. Readings of 30 degrees below zero are common in winter. The first fall frost can come to this area as early as late August and is certain to come by the first week of September; the last frost may be as late as the first week of June. Summers can be hot, though, with prolonged periods of 90-degree weather, since the cooling sea breezes that moderate temperatures in the coastal areas are not an influence here.

This section of Maine shares borders with the state of New Hampshire and the Canadian province of Quebec. Amity exists between Canada and Maine, with citizens of both countries regularly crossing the border for social, economic, and recreational purposes. People hiking in inland Maine may find it worthwhile to schedule time for a side trip to Canada. Many of the small Canadian towns retain their original ethnic characteristics and are pictures of the French-Canadian tradition that has continued for centuries.

HIKE 1 *MOUNT KATAHDIN VIA THE KNIFE EDGE*

General description: A day hike to the top of Mount Katahdin along a granite ridge called the Knife Edge.

General location: Mount Katahdin is in the southern part of Baxter State Park, in Piscataquis County, central Maine. The trailhead is a 45-minute drive from the town of Millinocket.

Maps: The Appalachian Mountain Club offers a map of Mount Katahdin and Baxter State Park; see also DeLorme's *The Maine Atlas and Gazetteer*, Maps 50 and 51.

Degree of difficulty: Strenuous. The trail is steep and rocky, with exposure to severe weather conditions possible even in summer. The Knife Edge, a granite ridge connecting Pamola and Baxter peaks, is 1 mile long with abrupt drop-offs on either side.

Length: 9.5-mile loop.

Elevations: Pamola Peak is 4,902 feet, and Baxter Peak is 5,267 feet.

Water availability: Bear Brook on the Helon Taylor Trail.

Special attractions: One of the most spectacular and breathtaking hikes in the East, with views of Moosehead Lake, the Penobscot River, and the mountains and hills in Acadia National Park and Camden Hills State Park. Mount Katahdin is the northern terminus of the Appalachian Trail.

Best season: May through October, weather permitting.

For more information: Baxter State Park, 64 Balsam Drive, Millinocket, ME 04462; (207) 723-5140.

Finding the trailhead: From points south take Interstate 95 north to the Medway exit. From Medway take Maine Route 157 west to Millinocket. Upon entering Millinocket, you will get your first close-up view of Mount Katahdin. From Millinocket, follow the signs to Baxter State Park. After entering the park at Togue Pond, bear right and head for Roaring Brook Campground. The hike begins at the ranger station. All hikers must register there, signing in and out. The park charges an out-of-state entry fee at the gate. It is advisable to arrive *early*. Campgrounds can be full, and trails are sometimes closed, so hikers have time to get back to the trailhead by nightfall.

The hike: Mount Katahdin can be hiked in a day by using several trails. The most exciting route goes along the Knife Edge, a granite ridge connecting Pamola and Baxter Peaks. Do not attempt to cross the Knife Edge if the weather turns foul; head back down instead and try again some other day. High winds can disrupt your footing, and snow or sleet can make the hike across the narrow ridge too dangerous. Electrical storms should also be a deterrent. Because of these hazards, park authorities may close the entire mountain or certain trails when dangerous conditions prevail.

The hike begins on the **Chimney Pond Trail** at the ranger station at Roaring Brook. Follow this trail for only a few hundred yards before

HIKE 1   MOUNT KATAHDIN VIA THE KNIFE EDGE

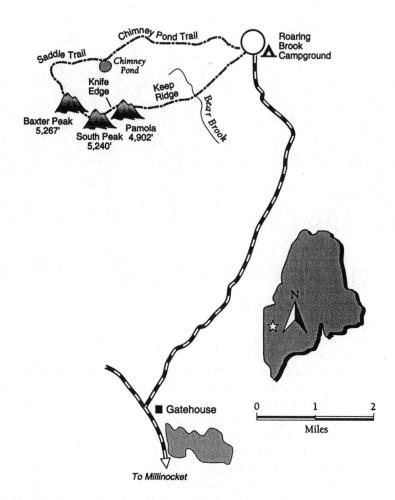

turning left on the **Helon Taylor Trail**. A few flat sections offer respite on this steep and rocky trail. You will need to use your hands to negotiate some of the boulders and ledges. Soon you will cross Bear Brook, the only water on the trail. From here on, the trail climbs Keep Ridge. After passing the tree line, you will see the serrated Knife Edge. More steep climbing brings you to the summit of Pamola, where you can see your route to Baxter Peak.

Some of the more difficult bouldering and scrambling occurs as you go down and up from the Chimney, between Pamola and Chimney peaks. Beyond that, the walking is still rugged on a narrow trail. The steepest cliffs on the north side make a huge glacial cirque containing Chimney Pond. At South Peak, the trail turns north and is not as exposed to winds.

A plaque at the summit announces Mount Katahdin as one terminus of the Appalachian Trail. On the opposite end of the trail is Springer

Small pond in Baxter State Park with Mount Katahdin in background.

Mountain, Georgia, more than 2,000 trail miles south.

From the summit, the trail to Chimney Pond heads northwest, where the **Cathedral Trail** branches off to the right. This trail is spectacular but also very steep, and the descent will be difficult because of the workout you just had. Instead of taking this trail to Chimney Pond, just keep going and take the easier **Saddle Trail** down. Two rock pinnacles jutting out into the cirque give the trail its name. They offer a good place to take a breather.

After reaching Chimney Pond, sign the hiker register at the ranger station. You can get a good perspective of your hike by consulting the relief model of the mountain and its trails found on the station's porch. The 3.3-mile Chimney Pond Trail back to Roaring Brook is not too steep, offering welcome relief to tired legs.

Baxter State Park includes more than 200,000 acres. The park was created through a series of gifts from former Maine governor Percival Baxter, beginning in 1931. Baxter inserted a condition that the park "shall forever be left in its natural wild state, forever be kept as a sanctuary for wild beasts and birds and forever be used for public forest, public park, and public recreational purposes." To this day, the park remains in wilderness condition. Primitive camping is allowed, although regulations prohibit pets, oversized vehicles, airplanes, motorboats, motorcycles, and all-terrain vehicles.

HIKE 2 *BIGELOW RANGE*

General description: A long day hike traversing the heart of the Bigelow Range, including the 4,150-foot summit of West Peak.

General location: East of the town of Stratton, between Flagstaff Lake and Maine Routes 16/27. Near Sugarloaf Mountain Ski Area in Franklin and Somerset counties in western Maine.

Maps: Appalachian Mountain Club *Maine Mountain Guide*, and DeLorme's *The Maine Atlas and Gazetteer*, Map 29.

Degree of difficulty: Difficult. The trail is strenuous, steep, and long with significant elevation gain.

Length: 12 to 15 miles round-trip, depending on where you begin and what side trips you take.

Elevations: 1,300 to 4,150 feet.

Water availability: No dependable water.

Special attractions: Lengthy ridge walks and fine views, as well as strenuous hiking in a limited alpine environment.

Best season: May through October, weather permitting.

For more information: Appalachian Mountain Club, 5 Joy Street, Boston, MA 02108; Maine Appalachian Trail Club, Box 283, Augusta, ME 04330; Maine Department of Conservation, State House Station 22, Augusta, ME 04333; (207) 287-3821.

Finding the trailhead: From Stratton, head southeast toward Sugarloaf Mountain Ski Area. Turn left onto an unmarked gravel road 4.5 miles west of the ski area on Maine Routes 16/27; proceed 1 mile to the Appalachian Trail (AT) crossing, then drive 0.6 mile to the road's end at a small parking area on Stratton Brook Pond. This road has some rough sections and may be difficult for two-wheel-drive vehicles. You may wish to leave your vehicle alongside the road when you find the going difficult and walk the rest of the way to the trailhead. Alternately, you could begin the hike from ME 16/27 and follow the AT in.

The hike: From the parking area, walk across the outlet of Stratton Brook Pond and follow the logging road. Bear left on this road at an old parking area. A little later, bear right at a fork. Signs exist at both points.

At this fork, the road becomes the **Firewarden's Trail**, a footpath with blue blazes. From here, it is an easy 1.4-mile climb to the junction with the **Horns Pond Trail**. Bear left on the Horns Pond Trail, which rises steeply. Soon you will pass a small pond and reach views of South Horn and Sugarloaf Mountain.

At the junction with the AT, turn right for the Horns Pond shelter, South Horn, West Peak, and Bigelow Col. From the shelter, the trail climbs steeply for 0.6 mile to the top of South Horn, where you can enjoy fine views to the south. If you have the energy, a side trip to the North Horn, 0.2 mile, is worth the effort. The view of Flagstaff Lake, an impoundment formed on the Dead River, is superb.

HIKE 2   BIGELOW RANGE

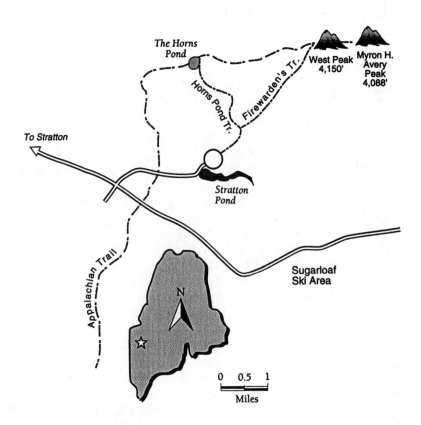

A forested ridge leads from South Horn to West Peak and its dramatic rocky profile. The trail follows this ridge, affording only limited views. West Peak and the other summits are all exposed, and low temperatures coupled with strong winds can cause hypothermia if you do not take precautions.

Descend from West Peak to Bigelow Col, where you can camp at a Forest Service campsite if you wish. From here, take the Firewarden's Trail back to the trailhead. If you still have plenty of energy, or if you are going to camp, you might want to climb Avery Peak. It is 0.4 mile to the fire tower on Avery Peak from the col. The walk down the Firewarden's Trail is very steep at first, but soon becomes more manageable with a less severe grade.

The 33,000-acre Bigelow Mountain Preserve is another example of the willingness of Maine's people to save the state's natural resources from unrestrained development. Plans for a huge ski complex here were dashed forever when a public referendum established the preserve in 1976.

HIKE 3 *GULF HAGAS*

General description: A hike along a gorge with steep cliffs and waterfalls.
General location: Northwest of the town of Milo in Piscataquis County.
Maps: DeLorme's *The Maine Atlas and Gazetteer*, Maps 41 and 42; see also the Maine Appalachian Trail Club *Guide to the Appalachian Trail in Maine*.
Degree of difficulty: Moderate.
Length: 6.5 miles round-trip.
Elevations: No significant elevations encountered.
Water availability: You will have access to several streams as well as the West Branch of the Pleasant River. If you do not have a purification system, bring your own water.
Special attractions: This beautiful canyon and the land around it was proclaimed a national landmark in 1968. As such, it is off-limits to logging. This hike takes place in the Katahdin Iron Works Multiple Use Forest. The Katahdin Iron Works itself has been preserved as a state historic memorial. You can walk around the old smelter and beehive charcoal burner. Informational signs explain the processes that took place on this site more than 100 years ago.

A primitive campsite in the multiple use forest serves as a base camp for those wishing to spend more than a day in the area.

For more information: Appalachian Mountain Club, 5 Joy Street, Boston, MA 02108; Maine Appalachian Trail Club, Box 283, Augusta, ME 04330.
Finding the trailhead: From Bangor, take Interstate 95 north to Howland and get off at Exit 54. From there, take Maine Route 6 to Milo. From Milo, take Maine Route 11 to Brownville Junction. About 5.5 miles north of Brownville Junction, watch for cultivated fields on the right and a good gravel road on the left. A large sign points the way to Katahdin Iron Works. Take this road, being certain to give logging trucks the right-of-way at all times.

Follow Katahdin Iron Works Road for 6.8 miles to the old iron works, on the right. A small caretaker's building is on the left, and ahead is a bridge over the West Branch of the Pleasant River. Park in front of the caretaker's building and pay $4 to the attendant. Ask about current road conditions as well as the height of the river.

Pass the gate, drive over the bridge, and watch for a right turn. After turning, go 3.5 miles, then bear left at a fork and go across another bridge over the West Branch of the Pleasant River. Here is a primitive campground, your base camp if you plan on staying. At 7 miles from the iron works, the Appalachian Trail (AT) crosses the road. Continue up a hill, where you might want to stop and take in the view. Go down the hill and, at 14 miles from the iron works, cross the West Branch of the Pleasant River one more time. Park on the left, well off the road, for your own safety and the safety of others. This is the trailhead.

The Katahdin Ironworks on the way to the trailhead for Gulf Hagas.

The hike: Walk up the road and watch for a trail marked with blue blazes on the right. Take this trail, and at 0.5 mile you will see Lloyd Pond on the left. You might want to take the side trail leading to the pond for a quick look.

Back on the main trail, continue on, watching for bits of old telephone wire sticking out of the ground. You are now on **Pleasant River Road**, although it is hardly a road as such. Cross a small stream at 1.1 mile and take a right turn. The trail becomes a bit steeper and bears to the left. Here, a small sign directs you to Gulf Hagas and the **Gulf Hagas Trail**.

Now the trail heads downhill and leads you to the head of the gulf, a pool with a single, rocky island. Here the walking is a bit difficult because of the unevenness of the ground. You will have to negotiate a number of large boulders and steep drops, but this can be done safely if you take your time.

Soon you will come to where a pair of river channels meet, at Billings Falls. You can dip your feet in the pool, but swimming may be risky business. After your break, continue down the trail to Stair Falls and on to the Jaws, a frothy, foaming constriction of the river.

Continue past the Jaws, and, at 3.1 miles, you will find yourself at Hammond Street Pitch. The sheer walls here reminded the old river drivers of a steep street in Bangor of the same name. Imagine yourself participating in a log drive through this place!

Walk past the pitch and bear left on a fork in the trail. This takes you

HIKE 3 GULF HAGAS

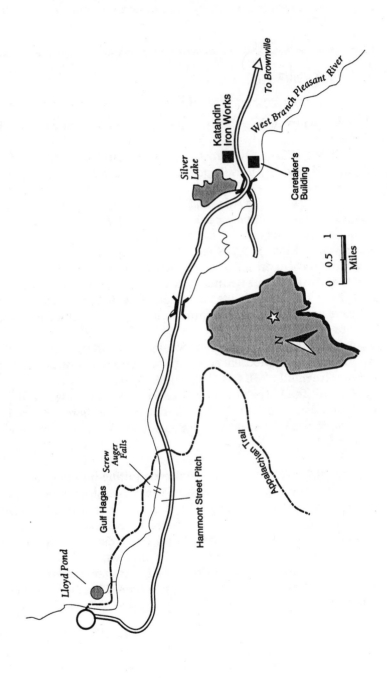

back on the Pleasant River Road. Walk along this road for 2.4 miles and you will come to the place where you turned off to go down to Gulf Hagas. From here, walk the same route you used to come in and return to the trailhead.

HIKE 4 *MOUNT KINEO*

General description: A hike to the top of a mountain that can only be reached by water.
General location: Diagonally across the water from Rockwood, a small village about halfway up Moosehead Lake's western shore in Somerset County.
Maps: DeLorme's *The Maine Atlas and Gazetteer*, Maps 40 and 41.
Degree of difficulty: Relatively easy.
Length: 4 miles round-trip.
Elevations: Mount Kineo is 1,789 feet above sea level.
Water availability: No drinking water. Bring your own.
Special attractions: Mount Kineo has cliffs that are composed of a particular type of flint that Native Americans traveled great distances to obtain. Objects constructed of this flint have been found at locations far removed from Mount Kineo.
Best season: May through November, weather permitting.
For more information: Moosehead Lake Region Chamber of Commerce, P.O. Box 581, Greenville, ME 04441; (207) 695-2702.
Locating the trailhead: Take Maine routes 6 and 15 to Rockwood. If you have a boat, you can launch at the new public landing there. Otherwise, you can find various outfitters and individuals who offer water taxi service to the trailhead.

The hike: Mount Kineo rises from a peninsula jutting into the middle of Moosehead Lake, the largest lake east of the Mississippi River that is contained within the bounds of a single state. It is a one-of-a-kind experience to climb a mountain that is situated in the middle of an inland sea surrounded by Maine's big woods. From the dock, you can take the shorter and steeper **Indian Trail**, about 1 mile long, which skirts the cliffs, or the slightly longer but less steep **Bridle Trail**, less than 2 miles long. An abandoned fire tower rests at the top of the mountain. There are fine views in all directions.

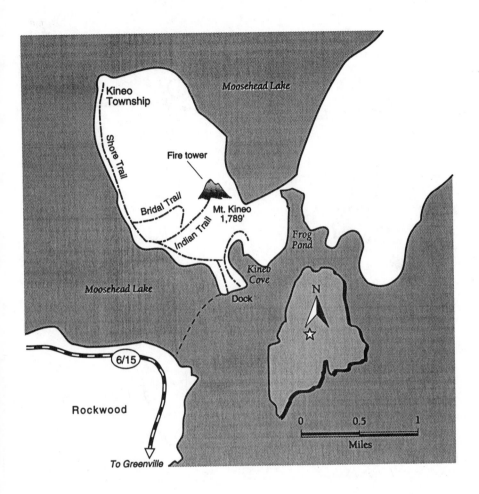

HIKE 5   *CARIBOU BOG*

General description: A hike through woodlands and freshwater marshes close to an urban area.
General location: Near Bangor and Orono in Penobscot County.
Maps: DeLorme's *The Maine Atlas and Gazetteer*, Map 23.
Degree of difficulty: Easy.
Length: 10 miles round-trip.

HIKE 5 CARIBOU BOG

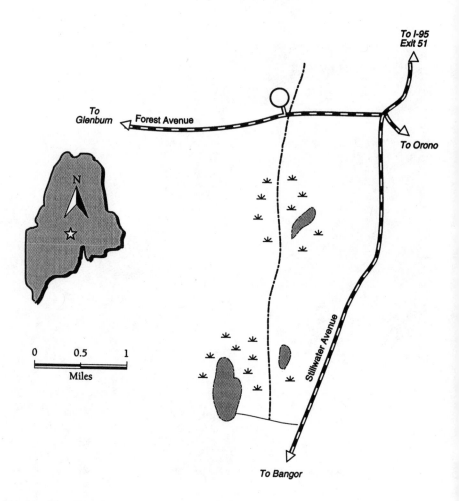

Elevations: No significant elevations encountered.

Water availability: Bring your own water.

Special attractions: This hike is popular with local residents because it leads through truly wild country, yet is within a few miles of a major city. Wildlife watchers can see deer, bear, coyotes, foxes, and a variety of songbirds and waterfowl.

Best season: Anytime except early spring, when the trail is too wet for comfortable hiking.

For more information: Consult DeLorme's *The Maine Atlas and Gazetteer* to see where you are in relation to other bogs and wetlands in the area.

Finding the trailhead: From Bangor take Stillwater Avenue north to the intersection of Forest Avenue in Orono. Turn right on Forest Avenue and park on the right by the entrance road for the Orono landfill. The trail begins on the left side of the road, across from the landfill entrance.

End of hike at Caribou Bog Trail.

The hike: Walk in from the trailhead at Forest Avenue. The trail is wide with a few wet spots, so wear rubber boots in the spring or after a rain. For the first mile, the trail is straight, passing a forest of firs, spruces, and white pines. At 1 mile, a large boulder on the right is worth investigating, since it is covered with a variety of lichens and mosses.

Just past the boulder, to the left of the trail, the first freshwater marsh begins. In spring and early summer you will be serenaded by a cacophony of bird songs and frog trills. As you continue, the land to the right of the trail turns to sphagnum bog, with typical bog plants and larch trees. Do not walk out on this ground, since it is only held above water by a thin layer of roots and plants and is a fragile environment.

Past the sphagnum bog, the trail goes through mixed forests with some large oak trees. At 2.5 miles, the trail leaves the wetlands and bogs and crosses a small stream in an upland woods.

At 4.5 miles, the trail forks. Bear right here. The trail begins to curve to the right, then to the left. You will be able to see an open area past the woods, far to the right. This is the beginning of the large bog at the end of the trail. At 4.8 miles, the trail becomes a built-up roadway with water on both sides. At 5 miles, the trail ends at a washout. A stream flows from east to west and enters a small pond in the center of the bog. This is a good spot to get photos of waterfowl. Past the washout, the trail goes through private property.

Use the same route to return to the trailhead.

HIKE 6 *BORESTONE MOUNTAIN*

General description: A half-day hike to an exposed mountain summit in a National Audubon Society sanctuary.
General location: North of the town of Monson in Piscataquis County, central Maine.
Maps: DeLorme's *The Maine Atlas and Gazetteer*, Map 41.
Degree of difficulty: Moderate. Some scrambling and handhold use required.
Length: 5 miles round-trip.
Elevations: The summit is 1,947 feet above sea level.
Water availability: Bring your own canteen for the hike.
Special attractions: Borestone is an impressive mountain with fine views in all directions. The trail is near a number of other places of interest, including Big Wilson Cliffs, Little Wilson Falls and Gorge, the Appalachian Trail, Barren Mountain, Slugundy Falls, and Moosehead Lake. Nearby Greenville has ample accommodations for those wishing to spend time in the area, sampling the various hikes.
Best season: May through November.
For more information: Sanctuary Manager, Sunrise Pond Audubon Visitor Center, P.O. Box 112, Monson, ME 04464. During summer season call (207) 661-4050.
Finding the trailhead: From Monson, take Maine routes 6 and 15 north to Elliotsville Road, on the right. Continue on Elliotsville Road for 7.8 miles to a bridge over Big Wilson Stream. Turn left immediately past the bridge and cross the Canadian Pacific Railroad tracks. The trailhead is 0.1 mile past the railroad tracks and is well marked. Park across the road from the trailhead, being sure to leave your vehicle out of the way of traffic.

The hike: Beginning at the trailhead, walk on a well-graded road for about 1.3 miles. The road steadily gains altitude, going through a series of switchbacks, until it reaches the National Audubon Society Visitor Center near Sunrise Pond. Stop here and pay an entry fee for using the area: $2 for adults, $1 for students, and no charge for children under 6 years of age (group rates available). You might also want to check out the natural displays at the center. Audubon rules dictate that no pets, firearms, camping, or fires are permitted.

From the center, follow a trail that crosses the outlet of Sunrise Pond (at the pond's southeastern end). The trail turns north and east, becoming rough, slippery, and a bit eroded. You will probably have to use your hands at the steepest sections. At 1.75 miles beyond the pond, you reach West Peak. For different views from East Peak, continue for 0.25 mile, where the trail leads down to a saddle and then climbs a barren ledge. From here, you can look down on Lake Onawa and to 2,660-foot Barren Mountain, on the other side of the lake. Return to the trailhead by the same route.

HIKE 6 BORESTONE MOUNTAIN

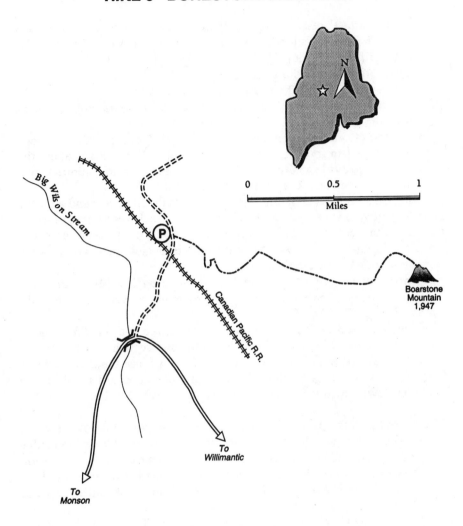

0   0.5   1

Miles

Big Wilson Stream

P

Canadian Pacific R.R.

Boarstone
Mountain
1,947

To
Willimantic

To
Monson

HIKE 7 *LEONARD'S MILLS*

General description: A hike on a self-guided nature trail through an experimental forest, starting from a restored eighteenth-century logging community.

33

General location: In Bradley, across the Penobscot River from Orono in central Maine.

Maps: The Maine Forest and Logging Museum has a map of the nature trails at Leonard's Mills; see also DeLorme's *The Maine Atlas and Gazeteer*, Map 23.

Degree of difficulty: Easy.

Length: 3.7 miles on various trails.

Elevations: No significant elevations encountered.

Water availability: Water is available from a hand-operated pump near the caretaker's house.

Special attractions: The Penobscot Experimental Forest practices ecology research, long-term forest management, and silviculture. Signs along the Nature Trail provide visitors with valuable information about forest management practices, forest types, and natural history.

Leonard's Mills hosts Living History Days on the first weekend after the Fourth of July and the first weekend in October each year. Living history volunteers present an accurate representation of the lifestyles in an early-American logging community. Leonard's Mills is always open to foot traffic.

Best season: May through October.

For more information: Maine Forest and Logging Museum, Inc., Museum Offices, 5768 South Annex A, University of Maine, Orono, ME 04469-5768; (207) 581-2871.

Finding the trailhead: From Orono, head south to Brewer. From there, take Maine Route 178 north and turn left at the intersection of Maine routes 178 and 9. Go about 2.5 miles on ME 178, and, just past the Bradley town line, look for a white sign on the right, directing you to Leonard's Mills. Drive 1.3 miles down the gravel road to the parking lot, which is the trailhead.

The hike: From the parking lot, walk past the gatepost and down the hill toward the covered bridge and water-operated sawmill. Cross the bridge and walk by the mill pond to the right. Continue to the old dam, where you will see several authentic bateaus stored. Walk past the bateaus and look for a sign for the **Nature Trail**, to the right of the blacksmith shop and hovel. Pick up a trail map from the box by the trail sign.

From the sign, walk in the woods on the Nature Trail. The trail follows Blackman Stream, although you will not get a good look at the stream and surrounding wetlands for a while. At 0.8 mile, the **White Trail** enters from the left. Continue straight on the Nature Trail. At 1 mile, cross a rustic wooden bridge over a stream and wetland and bear right on the **Red Trail**.

The Red Trail takes you on a signed loop through a woodland preserve and arrives back at the footbridge at 2 miles. From here, walk back on the Nature Trail and turn right on the White Trail. The White Trail takes you through a damp forest of spruce and fir. The trail crosses some wet areas, which you may have to skirt. Look for moose tracks in the mud. The White Trail becomes a bit obscure, but orange flagging indicates your direction. Keep bearing left, following the flagging, and at 3.4 miles, the White Trail rejoins the Nature Trail. Walk back through Leonard's Mills, cross the covered bridge, and return to the trailhead at 3.7 miles.

HIKE 7   LEONARD'S MILLS

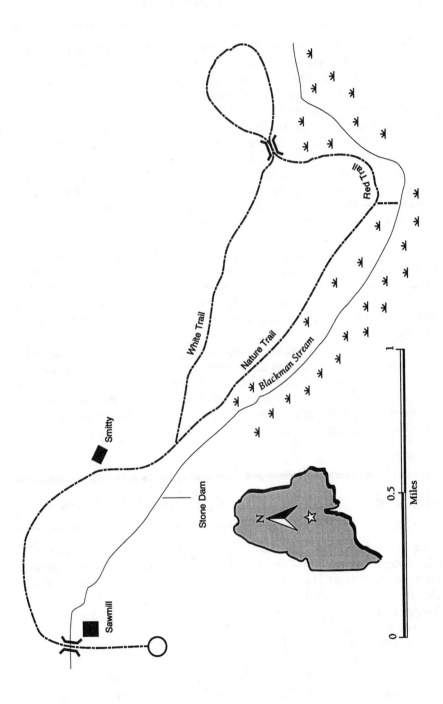

MIDCOAST HIKES OVERVIEW

Between Brunswick and Bucksport, the Maine coast is lined with historic towns and villages, small farms, rolling hills, and well-manicured fields. The region also holds a great many lakes, ponds, beaches, pine and spruce forests, freshwater and saltwater marshes, and mountains.

Most seed catalogues list coastal Maine as being in hardiness zone 5, with minimum temperatures of 20 degrees below zero. On the average this is true, but exceptionally cold winters can bring temperatures down to 30 degrees below zero. Of course, the opposite can also happen; a mild winter here can pass with no more than three or four days that the mercury drops into the negative scale. Summer temperatures in this part of Maine are usually 5 to 10 degrees milder than farther inland, but even here an occasional heat wave can keep temperatures in the 90s for several days in a row.

Coastal Maine is a seafood lover's paradise. Markets, restaurants, and vendors selling out of vans and pickup trucks offer such treats as fresh Maine lobster, soft-shell clams, Maine shrimp (smaller but sweeter than fantail or jumbo shrimp), and a variety of fin fish, including cod, pollock, hake, flounder, mackerel, and bluefish. Hikers can eat well in this part of the state.

Midcoastal Maine also drips with history, with forts built by the early colonists for protection from the French and Indians and rotting hulks of wooden vessels abandoned in harbors and coves. Its villages provide a touch of the old country: narrow streets above a harbor, gulls standing one-legged on a roof of native slate. Bring your camera when you hike and travel in this picturesque region.

HIKE 8   *UNITY STATION TO BURNHAM JUNCTION*

General description: A hike along a railroad line, passing through woods and along a lakeshore, a stream, a river, and several freshwater marshes.
General location: The town of Unity in the northern section of Waldo County, central Maine.
Maps: DeLorme's *The Maine Atlas and Gazetteer*, Maps 21 and 22.
Degree of difficulty: Easy.
Length: 9 miles one way.
Elevations: No significant elevations encountered.
Special attractions: This hike shows you a representative sampling of rural Maine countryside, just as taking a ride on a train is a good way to really see the country. You may see woodcutters using one of the private

Railroad trestle at Unity Pond.

crossings on their way to the woods, and you could walk past fishermen sitting on the edge of the railbed trying to catch enough perch for their supper.

In addition, the Belfast & Moosehead Lake Railroad operates a steam locomotive on this line, a rare sight nowadays. Bring your camera to capture this essence of the early days of railroading. The train signals at all crossings and is quite loud, so you should not have any trouble staying out of its way. Hearing-impaired persons should not do this hike alone.

Best season: You can hike here any time, but late September through mid-October is the most spectacular season because of colorful foliage. If you come in spring or summer, bring insect repellent.

Water availability: No potable water on the hike, but water is available at the station.

For more information: Belfast & Moosehead Lake Railroad, 1 Depot Square, Unity, ME 04988; (207) 338-2330. For more information about hiking railroad lines, write to the Maine Operation Lifesaver Committee, Bangor & Aroostook Railroad Company, Rural Route 2, Box 45, Bangor, ME 04401.

Locating the trailhead: From Belfast, take Maine Route 137 west to the intersection with Maine Route 220. Turn right on ME 220, and go 7 miles to the intersection with Maine Route 139. Turn left, cross the railroad tracks and look for Unity Station on the immediate right. The station is the trailhead.

The hike: Leaving the station, head west on the edge of the tracks. Just after walking past a field you will see the first road crossing. Unity Pond

HIKE 8   UNITY STATION TO BURNHAM JUNCTION

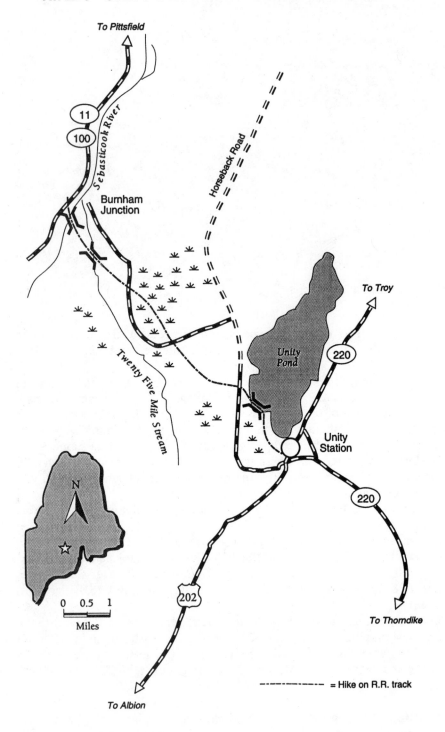

To Pittsfield

Sebasticook River

11

100

Burnham
Junction

Horseback Road

To Troy

Unity
Pond

220

Twenty Five Mile Stream

Unity
Station

220

N

To Thorndike

0   0.5   1

Miles

202

------------- = Hike on R.R. track

To Albion

comes into view on the right. A large freshwater marsh on the left is separated from the pond by the roadbed. Cross a metal trestle at the end of the marsh.

Now go through a forest of mixed softwoods and hardwoods. A hayfield on the left marks the beginning of a long bend in the tracks. After the bend you come to a straightaway, where you can see ahead for a considerable distance. At the end of the straightaway, the roadway bends again and comes to a 1.5-mile straightaway. Poplars and oaks line the tracks here. At the end of this straightaway, walk through a handsome stand of white birches, near a switch, and pass a private crossing.

Next you will come to another crossing, this time a hardtop road with a few small houses on either side. The roadbed crosses a small pond on both sides of the track. After leaving the road crossing, go by a bog on the right. Dead trees stand in the water, indicating the relative youth of the bog. A small brook goes under the tracks.

Within another 0.5 mile from the small bog, a true wetland begins, with marsh grasses and lots of water, even in the dry season. The roadbed has been built up here, and the train must go slow through this area due to its fragile underpinning. A water-filled ditch lines the track on both sides. Here you can see a variety of puddle ducks, including wood ducks and black ducks.

After leaving the wetland, the roadbed goes through more mixed growth and soon comes to another hardtop road crossing. It then goes into another long straightaway with nothing but woods on either side. After leaving the woods, the railroad crosses a metal and granite bridge spanning Twentyfive Mile Stream. After the stream, you come to another unimproved crossing and another long straightaway. Soon the tracks bear to the left by a small field. From here, you can see a few farmhouses and an old cemetery on the right.

At the end of the curve, the tracks cross a metal trestle over the Sebasticook River, one of the few places in Maine where you can fish for black crappie. Now you are in Burnham Junction. You can see a grain tower on the left. The track forks; take the right leg of the fork, and you have reached the end of the hike. Either ride the train back or walk back the way you came. If you have access to two vehicles, you might leave one here before starting the hike and use that to get back to Unity Station.

HIKE 9 *BLUE HILL*

General description: A hike up a lone mountain to a fire tower with panoramic views.
General location: North of the town of Blue Hill in Hancock County, midcoast Maine.
Maps: DeLorme's *The Maine Atlas and Gazetteer*, Map 15.

HIKE 9 BLUE HILL

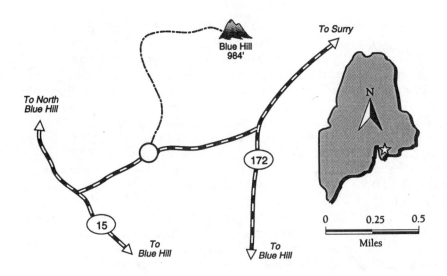

Degree of difficulty: Easy.
Length: 2 miles round-trip.
Elevations: 934 feet at the summit.
Water availability: Bring your own water.
Special attractions: Standing alone, Blue Hill was a landmark for mariners during the sailing age. It is near the historic village of Castine, as well as Deer Isle, a scenic island accessible by a bridge. The village of Blue Hill is a charming community, well worth a short visit.
Best season: April through October.
For more information: Check DeLorme's *The Maine Atlas and Gazetteer.*
Locating the trailhead: From Orland or Ellsworth follow U.S. Highway 1 east or west to Maine Route 15, also known as the Blue Hill Road. Follow ME 15 for about 11 miles and look for Mountain Road on the left. Follow Mountain Road for 0.4 mile and watch for a sign for the fire tower trail. The sign marks the trailhead.

The hike: The trail takes you through an open field and into a hardwood forest. The route gets steep, so be careful of footing on loose stones. Farther along, the trail bends to the northeast through thick fir and spruce. Looking west from a ledge near the trail, you can see Penobscot Bay, the Camden Hills, and Cape Rosier, as well as the towns of Castine, Brooksville, and Penobscot.

The trail finally climbs through the woods and ends at the summit where there is a fire tower. Looking south from here, you can see Blue Hill Bay. The hills and mountains of Mount Desert Island crop up from the east.

HIKE 10 *FRYE MOUNTAIN*

General description: A steep gravel trail leading to a fire tower at the summit of Frye Mountain in the Frye Mountain Game Management Area.
General location: About a half-hour drive from Belfast and the coast in midcoast Maine. Frye Mountain is located in Montville, an area of rolling hills and valleys in central Waldo County.
Maps: DeLorme's *The Maine Atlas and Gazetteer*, Map 14.
Degree of difficulty: Easy to moderate. This is a short trail, but fairly steep in its entirety.
Length: 0.3 mile one way.
Elevations: 1,139 feet at the summit.
Water availability: No potable water. Bring your own.
Special attractions: The view from the summit of Frye Mountain is excellent, offering scenes of the surrounding farmland, lakes, ponds, and a clear view of Penobscot Bay. The entire Frye Mountain Game Management Area is open to the public. Hunting and fishing are permitted.
Best season: May through November. Game Management Area roads are not plowed in the winter.
For more information: Maine Department of Inland Fisheries and Wildlife, 284 State Street, Station 41, Augusta, ME 04333; (207) 287-8000.
Finding the trailhead: From Belfast, head west on Maine Route 137 about 10 miles and turn left at Fosters Corner. Follow the unpaved Getchell Road about 3 miles, passing a metal gate, to where a sign indicates the trail to the fire tower. Park on the road next to the sign, leaving room for other vehicles to pass.

The hike: This public land was once private farmland, as old foundations, fields, and even an old cemetery here attest.

The trail is a wide, rocky path leading straight up to the fire tower. About halfway to the summit, the trail leads through a dense forest of balsam firs and hemlocks. Even in summer, this area is always cool and a good place to stop, rest, and catch your breath.

Just below the summit, the trail leads through a flat, grassy area. The rest of the way to the summit is over a granite ledge. Guardrails have been erected to assist you in scrambling over this ledge.

A Forest Service fire tower stands upon the summit. You can walk about on granite outcroppings at the summit. Lowbush blueberries grow here, as does a sprawling form of juniper. At one time, the distant outline of Mount Washington in the White Mountains of New Hampshire was visible on a clear day. Now, haze and air pollution originating in the Ohio River Valley make it impossible to see the distant peak.

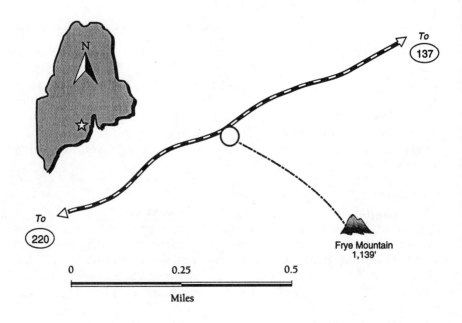

HIKE 11 *MOUNT WALDO*

General description: A hike up a mountain through blueberry fields and along rocky ledges.

General location: Midcoast Maine near the town of Frankfort in Waldo County.

Maps: DeLorme's *The Maine Atlas and Gazetteer*, Map 23.

Degree of difficulty: Easy, although the trail does cross several granite ledges, which can be slippery when wet.

Length: 2 miles round-trip.

Elevations: 1,064 feet at the summit.

Water availability: No water. The trail stays in the open, so bring your own supply if you are here on a hot day.

Special attractions: Mount Waldo granite was once the stock in trade of a thriving industry. Although granite is no longer quarried here, it can still be seen in buildings in many eastern cities, such as New York.

Mount Waldo is near Mendall Marsh,see Hike 19. These two hikes can easily be done in one day.

Best season: May through October.

For more information: DeLorme's *The Maine Atlas and Gazetteer*; the

Hazy vista from Mount Waldo Summit, looking southwest.

Appalachian Mountain Club's *Maine Mountain Guide.*

Finding the trailhead: Heading south from Bangor on U.S. Highway 1A, turn right on a paved road just past the Frankfort town office building. This road goes under a railroad overpass and up a short hill. Turn right after going 0.2 mile on this road, continuing to a fork in the road. Take the left branch of the fork. This unpaved road is rough but passable by two-wheel-drive vehicle, if you go slow. Early spring is not a good time to come here, because the road may be muddy and soft. Continue on this road for 1.6 miles to a metal gate on the left. Park off the road so as not to block the gate. This is the trailhead.

The hike: The gate should be open, but even if not, walk past it and go straight up the dirt road leading to the mountain. This road is bordered by blueberry land so, if you are sensitive to bee stings, be cautious, since blueberry growers often import hives of honeybees to assist in pollinating the blossoms. Stone fences divide the cultivated land, making the whole scene look like something out of the Scottish moors.

The dirt road goes straight from the gate to the base of the mountain. Here it bears to the right and then begins the actual ascent. Low-growing juniper and blueberries line the trail.

The trail becomes quite steep as the view of Swan Lake, the town of Monroe, and the rolling countryside to the west becomes more vivid. About halfway up the mountain, the trail goes over granite ledges. The view to the east and south comes into focus.

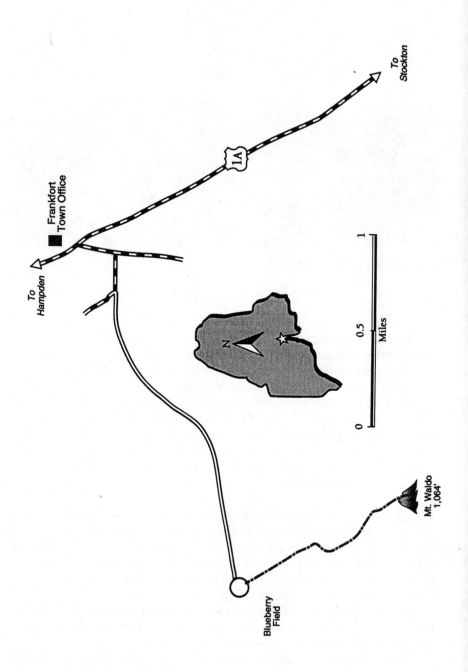

At the top, the ground is relatively flat. You can see the Penobscot River and the spires of the town of Winterport to the northeast, and Penobscot Bay to the south. One day I saw moose tracks in the lichen at the summit. The wonder is how the moose made it up there across the slippery granite ledge.

Bring insect repellent no matter when you come here. Wet areas on the summit are a haven for tiny but fierce mosquitoes.

HIKE 12 *FERNALDS NECK*

General description: A hike on a peninsula jutting into a scenic lake, a preserve held by The Nature Conservancy (TNC). The peninsula boasts cliffs and a large freshwater bog.

General location: Midcoast Maine, west of Camden in Waldo and Knox counties.

Maps: A map is available from the Maine Chapter of TNC, Fort Andross, 14 Main Street, Suite 401, Brunswick, ME 04011; (207) 729-5181. See also DeLorme's *The Maine Atlas and Gazetteer*, Map 14.

Degree of difficulty: Easy for the most part, but some scrambling is involved.

Length: 5 miles on various trails.

Elevations: No elevations encountered.

Water availability: No reliable water on trail. Bring your own.

Special attractions: Although Fernalds Neck is close to Camden Hills State Park, it is overlooked by the majority of hikers visiting the area. Here you can find peace and tranquillity, a natural area all to yourself.

Best season: Year-round, except in early spring, Maine's mud season, when the trails are very muddy.

For more information: Maine Chapter, TNC, Fort Andross, 14 Main Street, Suite 401, Brunswick, ME 04011; (207) 729-5181.

Finding the trailhead: Head north from Camden on Maine Route 52. Follow ME 52 to Youngtown Corner. From the corner, bear left and look for a small metal sign marking Fire Road 50, opposite highway marker 5016.

Turn down Fire Road 50 and go past the Hattie Lamb Fernald section of the preserve, which is on the left. The road turns to gravel past this section. Turn left at a fork in the road. If you come in mud season (not a good idea), the TNC preserve guide suggests you leave your vehicle here. Since there is practically no room to park, you would be better off to avoid this hike during the wet season. A small TNC sign confirms that you are heading in the correct direction.

Continue down this road and through a hayfield, where you will see a small parking area. A wooden box contains preserve guides, which you can return at the end of your hike. The parking area is the trailhead.

The hike: In 1969 Fernalds Neck was slated for destruction by housing developers. Instead of ruin, this beautiful natural area found salvation. The threat of development was sufficient to unite local residents to rally around the cause of preservation. Money was raised to purchase the property for the Maine Chapter of The Nature Conservancy (TNC), insuring that this beautiful natural area would be saved for all time. In 1979, 30 more acres were added to the preserve as the Hattie Lamb Fernald section, a gift from a Fernald descendant in memory of her mother. This unique natural area stands as a sign that our wild lands can and must be saved.

A short walk on an obvious trail through a small field will lead you to the wood's edge, where you will see a TNC sign near a stone wall. The trail goes through a break in the wall and through a stand of mature white pines. Walking is cushioned because the trail is covered with soft pine needles. Soon you will come to a sign indicating the **Orange Trail**. Go left on this trail.

A short distance down the trail you will see a sign for Balancing Rock, on the left. This huge mass of granite, as large as a dump truck, was left here by a glacier. Although the rock is not about to roll, only a small portion of it touches the ground. Walk back to the Orange Trail and continue on.

Soon, the trail makes a sharp switchback. From here, you can see the Great Bog. The trail heads downhill to a small wooden bridge. Bear right after crossing the bridge and follow the trail along the bog. At 0.8 mile, orange arrows indicate the beginning of the **Orange Loop**. Bear left. Here, the woods are a mixture of softwoods and oaks.

Balancing Rock at Fernalds Neck, Lincolnville.

HIKE 12   FERNALDS NECK

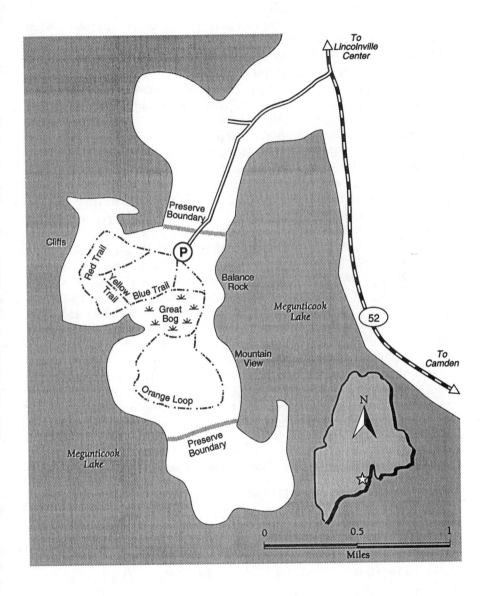

A trail on the left leads to some granite ledges on a cove of Megunticook Lake. From here, you can look directly across the lake to Maiden Cliff. The wooden cross on the cliff is plainly visible. After a rest, return to the Orange Loop.

The trail now winds the length of a rocky hillside, overgrown with stunted hemlock trees. Walking can be tricky here because of the boulders; a walking stick will be of great benefit. Now the trail heads straight uphill, next to a stone wall that marks the preserve boundary. The trail heads down the other side of the hill. You are now on the other side of the peninsula, and Megunticook Lake is again visible.

Now the hike calls for more scrambling over ledges and large granite boulders. Pass a rock-strewn cove on the left. The trail follows the edge of the bog and crosses a plank bridge. After walking 2.3 miles, you are once again at the beginning of the Orange Loop.

Head back north on the Orange Trail to the intersection of the **Yellow Trail**. Go left on the Yellow Trail to where the trail joins the **Blue and White Trail**. Bear left on the Blue and White Trail. This trail is narrow and rocky. Dense softwoods shade the forest floor here, even on a sunny day. At 0.2 mile, turn right on the Yellow Trail.

The Yellow Trail leads over a pine-studded ridge and turns to a narrow, mossy path. You have the feeling that you are walking through a tunnel, since the hemlocks are so dense on either side. The underbrush gives way to open, mature pines. It's easy to feel as if you are in a huge forest. You may want to stop here and take in the total quiet.

At the end of the Yellow Trail, turn left on the **Red Trail**. Follow it to the **Blue Loop Trail**. Go left at the Blue Loop Trail and you will come to the cliffs. Signs prohibit diving from the 60-foot cliffs, although you probably do not need to be told that to dive here would be foolhardy. If you brought lunch, this would be a good place to have it. Sit on the cliffs and watch for loons and ducks swimming below, or relax while you gaze at distant mountains across the lake. After lunch, retrace your steps to the Red Trail along the Blue Loop Trail. You have now walked 4 miles.

Continue north on the Blue Loop Trail. The woods here are mostly pine with some hemlocks and a few spruce. The trail narrows and goes over a corduroy bridge. This is a wet area in spring, even with the corduroy. Follow the signs back to the trailhead. You will have walked a total distance of 5 miles.

HIKE 13   *MOOSE POINT STATE PARK*

General description: A hike in an oceanside park with opportunities to walk along the water's edge and through cool piney woods.
General location: Just off U.S. Highway 1 between Belfast and Searsport in Waldo County.
Maps: DeLorme's *The Maine Atlas and Gazetteer*, Map 14.
Degree of Difficulty: Easy. This is a good starter hike if you are on the way to the Camden Hills or Acadia National Park.
Length: 1-plus-mile loop.
Elevations: No appreciable grades.
Water availability: No dependable water.
Special attractions: The park offers oceanside picnic tables and a chance to see a variety of sea creatures, including seals, porpoises, and birds such

HIKE 13 MOOSE POINT STATE PARK

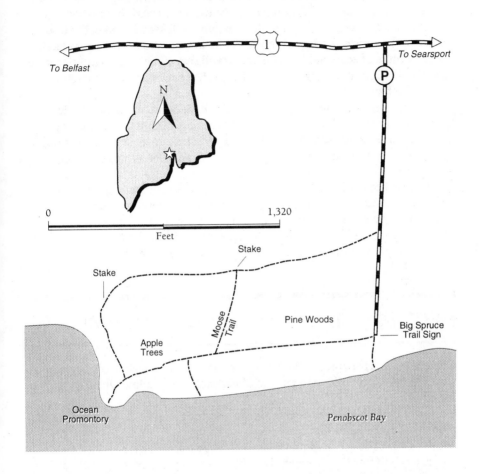

as double-crested cormorants, loons, sea ducks, bald eagles, and ospreys. Tidal pools, formed by retreating water at low tide, hold diverse marine organisms. This is a particularly fascinating hike for children.

Best season: All 12 months of the year.

For more information: Maine Department of Parks and Recreation, State House Station 22, Augusta, ME 04333; (207) 548-2882, or (207) 287-3821 off-season.

Finding the trailhead: From Belfast, head toward Searsport on U.S. Highway 1. Watch for the Moose Point State Park sign on the right, just past the town line in Searsport. The parking lot is the trailhead.

The hike: From the parking lot, walk down the main road, past the toll booth. At the end of the road you will come to a grassy area along the ocean, with picnic tables and paths leading to the shore. From here, you can see Sears Island to your left, Turtle Head on Islesboro Island out in front, and the Bluff in Northport to your right.

At the far right of the lower parking area is a sign for **Big Spruce Trail**. This should be called Big Pine Trail, since it goes through pine woods, with few spruce to be seen. Following the trail, you will see several paths leading to the rocky shore. At low tide the rocks are covered with rockweed, a slippery form of seaweed, so be careful walking. Rough benches are set up at various points along Big Spruce Trail, perfect for relaxing and looking out across the bay.

Continuing on, you will come to a small glade with a picnic table. The trail picks up on the far side of the glade and goes through a fragrant patch of sweet ferns. Follow the trail past some old apple trees in need of pruning until you come out at Moose Point. If the wind is onshore, there may be some surf.

Follow the trail from Moose Point through a handsome grove of white birches and watch for a gray painted post and a yellow flag on a tree. Take the trail to the right, through dense spruce growth, and you will come out to a wide path called the **Moose Trail**. Turn left on the Moose Trail and follow the path to the main road and back to your vehicle.

HIKE 14   *LAKE SAINT GEORGE STATE PARK*

General description: A hike up a small mountain overlooking an island-studded lake. The hike ends at the Sheepscot River, a favorite spot to fish for trout.

General location: Near Searsmont in western Waldo County across the road from Lake Saint George.

Maps: DeLorme's *The Maine Atlas and Gazetteer*, Map 13.

Degree of difficulty: No technical difficulty, but the first 0.9 mile of trail is very steep.

Length: 5.6 miles round-trip.

Elevations: Slight.

Water availability: Water is available at the park.

Special attractions: The park is located on a crystal-clear, spring-fed lake. It offers overnight camping, swimming, and fishing for brook trout, land-locked salmon, largemouth and smallmouth bass, and white perch. It's a good place to use as a base camp if you do other hikes in the Midcoast area. The Camden Hills are nearby, as are Moose Point State Park, Tanglewood, Leo's Trail, Ducktrap Harbor, and the Belfast and Moosehead Railroad line. Camden Hills State Park would serve the purpose as well, but Lake Saint George State Park is less crowded and located on a quieter road.

Best season: April through October.

For more information: Lake Saint George State Park, Liberty, ME 04909; (207) 589-4255.

Information sign at Lake Saint George State Park, Liberty.

Finding the trailhead: Take Maine Route 3 about 5 miles west of North Searsmont and watch for a wooden sign indicating Lake Saint George State Park. Park across from the sign in the day-use area and walk back across ME 3 to the park sign. The sign is the trailhead.

The hike: The forest around Lake Saint George is a mix of softwoods and hardwoods, with beeches being prominent. Moose and deer are sometimes seen on the trails, as are songbirds, woodcocks, and ruffed grouse. Loons swim on the lake, and their haunting cries can be heard in morning and evening.

Follow a well-marked trail uphill from the park sign. The first 0.5 mile of trail is steep, so take your time and save energy for the balance of the hike. The trails were first constructed as cross-country ski trails, but a system of hiking trails is now being developed. The ski trails leave and re-enter the hiking trails, inviting leisurely exploration. These ski trails are well-marked and can't be mistaken for the main trail.

The main trail bears left at the top of a small mountain and crosses a rough, wooden bridge. Continue on and look for the **Spruce Run** sign at an intersection. Bear left on Spruce Run for a short distance and look for a road to the right. Follow this road to a snowmobile trail that runs east and west. Alternately, you can continue on Spruce Run and walk a loop, which takes you through a magnificent spruce woods. The ground is lush with moss, lending enchantment to the atmosphere. After completing the loop, go back down the trail and take a right on the road, continuing to the snowmobile trail.

HIKE 14   LAKE SAINT GEORGE STATE PARK

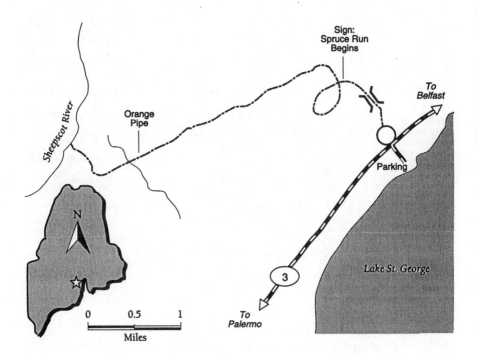

Go west on the snowmobile trail to where a wood road enters from the left. Take the right fork to where the trail crosses a deeply cut seasonal brook. Continue for 0.2 mile past the brook and follow a trail to your right, across from a sign prohibiting motorized vehicles. Follow this trail for 0.3 mile to the Sheepscot River. The distance from the trailhead to the river is 2.8 miles.

Walk back to the trailhead on the same route. Or take the snowmobile trail back to the fork and take a right, going up a steep hill to Lampson Road, a quiet country lane. Lampson Road goes down a hill and intersects Maine Route 3 at Shermans Corner. Turn right at Shermans Corner and follow ME 3 back to the park. The road follows the contour of Lake Saint George, making for a pleasant walk.

HIKE 15 *BELFAST TO WALDO STATION*

General description: A hike along a scenic railroad line, beginning on the shores of Belfast Harbor and ending at Waldo Station, an old-fashioned whistle stop.

General location: Between Belfast, on the coast, and Waldo, the first inland town west, in Waldo County.

Maps: DeLorme's *The Maine Atlas and Gazetteer*, Maps 14 and 22.

Degree of difficulty: Easy.

Length: 6.5 miles one way. Those wishing to hike farther along the railroad line have the initial 6.5 miles, plus 6 miles from Waldo to Brooks and another 12 miles to Burnham Junction.

Elevations: None encountered.

Water availability: Although the line generally follows Wescot Stream and is crossed by several lesser streams and brooks, none of these sources can be considered safe for drinking. Bring a canteen.

Special attractions: Several active beaver ponds and an excellent variety of wildlife, including bald eagles, ospreys, white-tailed deer, moose, ruffed grouse, woodcocks, and a variety of waterfowl and shorebirds.

Best season: Year-round, with migrating warblers in May, trout fishing in spring, and spectacular fall foliage in October.

For more information: Belfast & Moosehead Lake Railroad, 1 Depot Square, Unity, ME 04988; (207) 338-2330. A courtesy call is suggested for hikers; ask for a train schedule. More information, including helpful tips on hiking rail lines, is available from the Maine Operation Lifesaver Committee, Bangor & Aroostook Railroad Company, Rural Route 2, Box 45, Bangor, ME 04401.

Locating the trailhead: The hike begins at the train station located on the Belfast waterfront, just to the left of the public landing. Parking is available in the municipal parking lot, just off Main Street, up the hill from the landing.

The hike: Pick up the rail line at the Belfast waterfront. The line follows the Passagassawaukeag (local people call it the "Passy") River. At low tide, this river is reduced to a narrow channel, winding through mudflats and mussel beds. These mudflats provide income for people who dig marine worms for sale to bait shops up and down the east coast. Just outside town, the line passes a narrow point in the river, the site of a bridge that once connected East Belfast with Belfast proper. The old stone abutments remain, as do ancient wooden posts sticking out of the water, sentinels of the past. Double-crested cormorants often occupy the tops of these posts. During warm weather, the cormorants hold their wings aloft, as if to better allow the sea breezes to cool them down.

Just past the old bridge site, a sand spit known as the Beavertail juts out into the river. Black ducks swim around the edges of this spit, searching for any marine life that may have been dislodged by the swift tide. Mature and immature bald eagles and ospreys often cruise this section of the river.

HIKE 15 BELFAST TO WALDO STATION

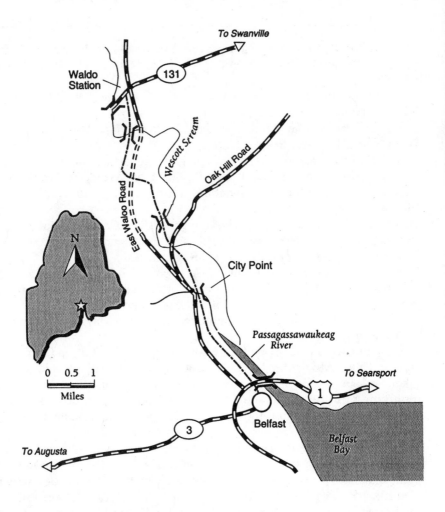

At approximately 1 mile from the trailhead, you will encounter a metal railroad bridge over the Passagassawaukeag River. This is City Point. In the summer, schools of menhaden converge just downstream from this bridge, herded by numbers of voracious striped bass. After the fall rains, Atlantic salmon can sometimes be seen beneath the bridge, on their way upstream to spawn.

Past the bridge, the line crosses a tarred road. Shortly after crossing the road, the line parallels Wescot Stream, a tributary of the Passagassa-waukeag. The line crosses this stream three times between here and the end of the hike. The balance of the hike is primarily through abandoned and working farmland. Ancient apple trees grow in profusion, offering wormy but chemical-free fruit to weary hikers. Much of the roadbed is

The Spirit of Unity, on B & ML Railroad line.

lined with wild raspberries and blackberries. If you hike here in the summer, you can eat your fill.

At any point of the hike you are liable to encounter a deer or moose. Keep a sharp lookout on the gravel roadbed for the tracks of these animals. Woodchucks can be seen sitting alongside their burrows in the fields, and in the evenings, woodcocks can be heard twittering. Loons sometimes use Wescot Stream as a travel route, so you may be fortunate enough to get a serenade.

If you have a ticket, you can ride the train back to Belfast after you have reached Waldo Station. The railroad people are willing to oblige hikers, and you can arrange to be let off or picked up at any point along the line.

HIKE 16   *BROOKS ESKER TO HALFMOON POND*

General description: A hike that begins at the end of a 0.6-mile-long esker and goes around a small lake, up a hill to a remote mountain pond, and back.
General location: Northwest of Belfast in Waldo County.
Maps: DeLorme's *The Maine Atlas and Gazetteer*, Maps 14 and 22.
Degree of difficulty: Easy.

Length: 3.8 miles round-trip.

Elevations: Slight.

Water availability: Although seasonal streams cross the trail, they are of questionable quality. Bring your own water.

Special attractions: The drive in to the trailhead takes you the entire length of an esker, a narrow ridge of sand and gravel formed during the last glacial period. After completing the main hike, you can explore the esker, noting its steepness and sandy deposits.

Halfmoon Pond is specially managed for brook trout. Carry a fishing rod if you come here in May or June, being sure to check current fishing regulations.

Best season: May through October.

For more information: Maine Department of Inland Fisheries and Wildlife, 284 State Street, Station 41, Augusta, ME 04333; (207) 657-4977.

Finding the trailhead: From Belfast, head north on Maine Route 7, also known as the Moosehead Trail. Turn left on Maine Route 131, by the Forest Service ranger station. Continue for 0.6 mile on ME 131 and turn right on Maine Route 203, directly across from a cornfield. Proceed 0.8 mile on ME 203. Look for a chicken barn and a large, light green farmhouse on the left close to the road.

Three dirt roads lead through the yard of the farm. Take the middle road and proceed past a fallen barn on the right. This is timber company land; logging trucks have the right of way. Proceed for 0.6 mile until you

HIKE 16 BROOKS ESKER TO HALFMOON POND

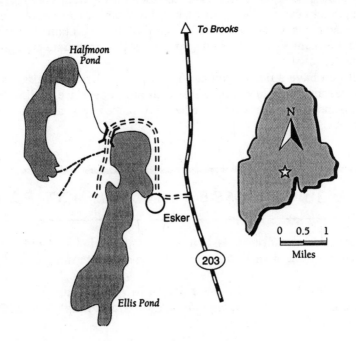

End of the trail at the head of Halfmoon Pond.

come to a sharp right turn by a lake. This is the trailhead. Park on the grass near the lake, making certain your vehicle is well off the road.

The hike: Follow the road you drove in on to a metal gate. Walk past the gate on the road. You will see Ellis Pond on your left. Continue walking as the road winds around the north end of the pond and heads south, still following the contour of the pond. The forest here is primarily fir, spruce, and hemlock. The area is frequented by moose, so keep an eye out for tracks.

After walking 1.1 miles, cross a rough wooden bridge, which goes over a stream entering Ellis Pond. This is a good spot to take a break. You can walk down the stream and sit on one of the large boulders at the stream mouth. If you come in the spring, watch the sandy bottom for schools of spawning perch.

Continue on the trail for another 0.4 mile, passing an old gravel extraction site on the right. The trail to Halfmoon Pond is on your right near a decaying pile of pine logs. An old beech tree, half dead with blight, is to the immediate right of the trail.

Take this narrow, rocky trail for 0.2 mile to a fork. Take the right-hand trail at the fork. Proceed for another 0.2 mile. The trail narrows and leads directly to the edge of Halfmoon Pond, a delightful mountain pond ringed with highbush blueberries. If you have time, walk around the pond. (It will take about an hour.) Otherwise, follow the same route back to the trailhead.

On the way back, you might wish to explore the left-hand trail at the fork. It leads through a recent chopping area and up the side of a small mountain. Do not do this in summer, since the trail is a jungle of briars, and deerflies are fierce. Spring and fall would be good times to walk to the top and check the view.

HIKE 17   *TANGLEWOOD*

General description: A hike to a small valley, along a trout and salmon river, through dense softwoods and over mature hardwood ridges.

General location: Near the town of Lincolnville near Penobscot Bay in Waldo County.

Maps: DeLorme's *The Maine Atlas and Gazetteer*, Map 14.

Degree of difficulty: Easy.

Length: 6 miles round-trip.

Elevations: No appreciable elevations encountered, although the trail has many short steep sections.

Water availability: Although the cottages at nearby Tanglewood 4-H Camp are supplied with water, these are not for public use. Several spring-fed streams cross the trail, but the integrity of the water may be questionable. For safety's sake bring your own.

HIKE 17   TANGLEWOOD

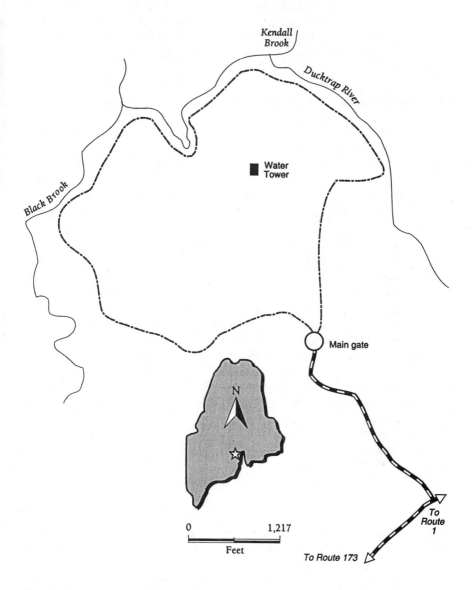

Special attractions: The Ducktrap River is one of a handful of streams that is host to an autumn run of Atlantic salmon, called "the king of game fish" by some. Special fishing regulations protect the salmon and native brook trout here.

Best season: Year-round.

For more information: Contact Leslie C. Hyde, Extension Educator, Knox-Lincoln County Extension office, 375 Main Street, Rockland, ME 04841; (207) 594-2104. Or call Jim and Cindy Dunham, Directors, Tanglewood 4-H Camp; (207) 789-5868.

Finding the trailhead: From Lincolnville Beach, go 0.9 mile north on U.S. Highway 1. Watch for painted wooden signs indicating Tanglewood 4-H Camp, on the left. Turn right on the hardtop Ducktrap Road and drive 0.7 mile to a gravel road on the right, where you will see another Tangle-wood 4-H Camp sign. Proceed 0.8 mile to a gate and parking area. The gate marks the trailhead.

The hike: Tanglewood 4-H Camp is a program of the University of Maine Cooperative Extension Service. The land is leased from the State of Maine, so the public is free to use the trails. The hike takes place in a hilly, sometimes dense forest. In winter, the trails are used for cross-country skiing and are renowned locally for their beauty and seeming remoteness.

Walk down the gravel road that leads downhill from the parking area. Take the first right-hand path. This is marked by a yellow arrow and a sign marking **Trail 1**. The trail goes steadily downhill for 0.6 mile, then levels off and goes straight through a boggy area. Your feet will stay dry if you stay on the corduroy bridge. Soon you will cross a log bridge over a deep, narrow, spring-fed brook. You will find a map of the area on your right.

At 0.8 mile you will come to a fork in the trail. Take the trail to the right, which goes through a pretty grove of mixed hardwoods: oaks, maples, and white birches. From here, the trail becomes narrow and heads down a steep hill. The trail makes a sharp left at the bottom of the hill. Here you will get your first view of the Ducktrap River.

Follow the trail along the river until you come to a sign that points to a ski shelter. Continue along the river to a bridge and go about 1 mile to the salmon pool, a favorite of local fishermen.

Bear left at a sign marking **Trail 6**. The trail crosses a wooden bridge and stops at another fork. Take the right fork and continue along the river through a small grove of planted white pine. Note the boxes nailed to trees at the river's edge. These are wood duck nesting boxes, which have helped save the colorful ducks from extinction.

As you walk on, you will see where a pine tree has fallen across the river, making a natural bridge suitable for raccoons but too risky for people. The trail goes up a steep grade. You will see a sign for the **Nature Trail** on the left. Go right here. At 3.7 miles, the trail goes through a wet area, full of tall marsh grasses. Bear right, and the trail will soon lead you to what appears to be an old wood road.

The road goes through an open wood of pines and oaks. At 4.4 miles, you will come to another fork. Trail 6 and **Trail 8** intersect here, marked by a small sign. Go left on Trail 6, proceeding through a thick hardwood stand. At 4.6 miles, you will come to a granite pillar near a fork in the road. Go right.

At mile 5, go straight past a trail at the right marked as Trail 8. The trail goes through a group of mature white pines as you continue. At 5.6 miles, you will come out on the gravel road leading back to the trailhead. Walk up the road; at 6 miles, you will be back at your vehicle.

HIKE 18 *LEO'S TRAIL*

General description: A walk through a woodlot and stands of fir and northern red oak.

General location: Near Lincolnville and Penobscot Bay in Waldo County.

Maps: DeLorme's *The Maine Atlas and Gazetteer*, Map 14.

Degree of difficulty: Easy to moderate. The trail goes downhill from the trailhead to its end at the Ducktrap River. A steep bank and large boulders must be negotiated at trail's end, however, in order to reach the riverbank.

Length: 0.6 mile one way, although the trail connects with the Tanglewood trail system at the river.

Elevations: The highest point is 200 feet above sea level.

Water availability: No potable water.

Special attractions: This trail explores a good example of a working woodlot, with some areas cleared of underbrush and some untouched in an ongoing selective cutting operation.

The Ducktrap River, at trail's end, has a population of native eastern brook trout. It is also an Atlantic salmon river. The larger fish ascend the river in the fall, but the smolts, or young fish, stay upstream all year. Fly-fishing is permitted; check regulations.

Best season: Year-round, except that fall foliage is so brilliant in this area that an autumn hike will be the most spectacular in terms of sheer beauty.

For more information: Leo T. Mills, P.O. Box 3, Lincolnville Beach, ME 04849; (207) 789-5461.

Finding the trailhead: From Lincolnville Beach, head east on U.S. Highway 1. After going 1 mile, turn left on Ducktrap Road and turn right at the first fork, going on to Tanglewood Road. At 0.6 mile from U.S. 1, look for a sign on the right that reads "Dunham." Turn right here and proceed for less than 0.1 mile. A small sign on left reads "Gitstuck Road." Less than 0.1 mile from Gitstuck Road, you will see another road on the left. Park on either side of this road, far enough out of the lane to permit a log truck to pass.

The hike: The trail winds through a lightning-prone area, with many lightning-struck trees showing the immense power of an electrical storm. Some trees are still standing; others are reduced to blackened, shattered stumps. **Do not** hike on this trail during stormy weather because of the extreme danger of a lightning strike.

From the trailhead, you will walk through sparsely wooded land, with some northern red oak evident. The trail is flagged. Your route heads downhill, making a gradual descent to the Ducktrap River. At the bottom of the first hill, the ground becomes moist and mossy because of seeping springs farther up the hillside. The flagged trail bends slightly north through dense stands of balsam fir and northern white-cedar, then bears west again, becoming steeper as it heads down to the banks of the river.

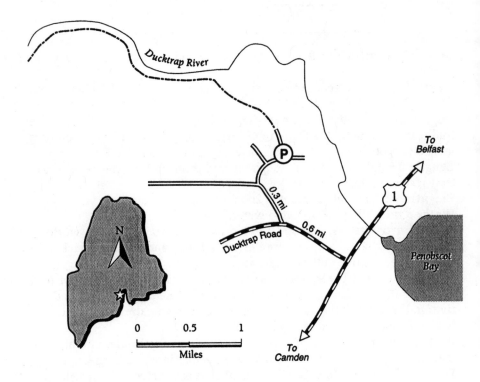

Watch your footing, since the ground is littered with dead leaves that are slippery when wet.

Upon reaching the river, do not go downstream, since that is private land. In summer and fall, the water is quite low, allowing you to cross the river in many places. Sit down for a few moments and watch for rising trout and salmon. White-tailed deer and moose may come to the river late in the afternoon. Bald eagles and ospreys are often seen cruising up and down the river. Bring your camera.

HIKE 19 *MENDALL MARSH*

General description: A hike through the 371-acre Howard Mendall Wildlife Management Area, a salt marsh bounded by a tidal river.
General location: Along U.S. Highway 1A just south of the village of Frankfort in Waldo County.
Maps: DeLorme's *The Maine Atlas and Gazetteer*, Map 23.
Degree of difficulty: Moderate. Walking through the marsh can be challenging because of numerous tidal streams. These channels, only 1 or

2 feet wide and up to 6 feet deep, are often obscured by marsh grasses.
Length: No marked trails. The length of the hike depends on how far the hiker wishes to go.
Elevations: No significant elevations.
Water availability: Bring your own water.
Special attractions: Waterfowl, shorebirds, and an active bald eagle nest.
Best season: April through November. October is insect-free and offers colorful foliage on all sides of the marsh.
For more information: Information and Education Division, Maine Department of Inland Fisheries and Wildlife, 284 State Street, Station 41, Augusta, ME 04333; (207) 547-4165.
Finding the trailhead: Follow U.S. Highway 1A south from Frankfort, looking for a sign on the left indicating a public boat launch. Go 0.5 mile past the boat launch and look for a sign indicating the Howard Mendall Wildlife Management Area on the left. A dirt road, passable by two-wheel-drive vehicles, goes to a small circle. The circle is the trailhead. Park off the road.

The hike: This hike is exciting because of its unstructured nature. You determine where and how far you will go.

Follow the dirt road to where it ends at a gravel pad surrounded by large granite boulders. Here, at the riverside, you can look up and down the shore, getting a good idea of the expanse of the marsh. The ground on both sides of the road is quite firm, so you might want to explore some of

A tidal stream retaining wall at low tide.

HIKE 19 MENDALL MARSH

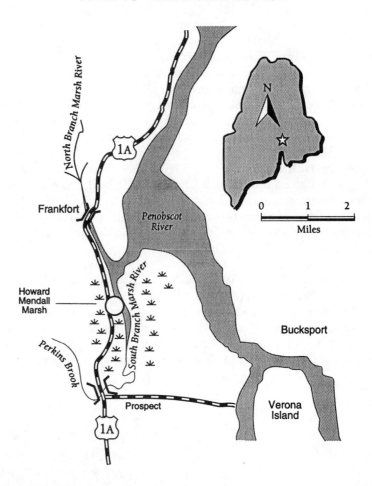

the tidal pools on either side. If you object to wet feet, wear rubber knee-length boots. On the way back to the trailhead, you will notice a large tidal stream. You can cross this stream from the south side of the circle, where it becomes narrow enough to jump over.

Heading south, you have a choice of following along the South Branch of the Marsh River, or staying in the middle of the marsh. Either way, you will find that you will need to retrace your steps, since the area abounds with cul-de-sacs formed by the numerous tidal streams.

As you walk along, be prepared to jump ducks from tidal pools. Often, you will not see these pools until you are quite near them, but the ducks will hear you coming before you see them. They can give you quite a start as they explode from the ground in front of you. Areas of short grass are home to smaller sora and larger Virginia rails and Wilson's snipe. You can easily spot a rail if you flush one because its legs hang down in flight. On the river you will see herring gulls, and, if you are lucky, an osprey or even a bald eagle. Shorebirds wade the mudflats at low tide, leaving identifiable tracks.

Although Mendall Marsh is bordered by U.S. Highway 1, you get a feeling of isolation and seclusion once you get into the marsh and along the river. The mountains on the other side of the highway and the hills across the river give you the impression that you are in a giant, grassy bowl.

HIKE 20 *ROCKLAND BREAKWATER*

General description: A walk on a granite breakwater to a lighthouse on Penobscot Bay.
General location: Jameson Point in the City of Rockland, Knox County.
Maps: DeLorme's *The Maine Atlas and Gazetteer*, Map 14.
Degree of difficulty: Easy in good weather, but may be dangerous during storms.
Length: 2 miles round-trip.
Elevations: Sea level.
Water availability: Bring your own water.
Special attractions: See marine birds and mammals, schools of migratory fish, and lobster fishermen at work. The Great Schooner Race takes place here each July, beginning at the island of North Haven and ending at Rockland Breakwater. Pleasure boats and commercial boats pass off the

View of the Rockland Breakwater. Note the four-masted schooner, middle left.

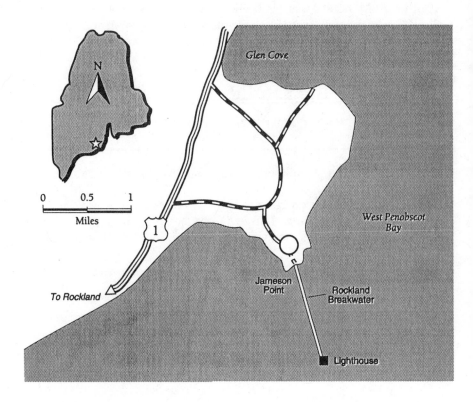

end of the breakwater, headed in and out of Rockland Harbor.

Best season: Year-round, but the rocks may be icy in winter.

For more information: Rockland/Thomaston Area Chamber of Commerce, (207)-596-0376.

Finding the trailhead: From U.S. Highway 1, just north of Rockland's business center, take Waldo Avenue. Go 0.5 mile and look for a sign for Shore Access Road on the right. Go 1.4 miles down Shore Access Road. Toward the end of the road, you will see the Samoset Resort golf course on the left. There is ample parking at the end of the road. The trailhead begins at a bronze plaque by the water. From the plaque, follow a gravel path along the shore to the beginning of the breakwater.

The hike: The hike takes you along the length of the breakwater to a lighthouse at the extreme end. The breakwater is composed of huge blocks of Maine granite, placed here in the 1880s to protect Rockland Harbor from the ravages of the Atlantic Ocean. A ramp leading to a float is on your right, partway out.

The breakwater is a popular fishing spot in the summer. Schools of mackerel, bluefish, and even striped bass pass by here. Cunners, fishes similar to tropical wrasses, live between cracks in the underwater boulders. These fish are able to crack periwinkles and other shellfish with their powerful teeth. Lobster buoys dot the water on both sides of the breakwater, and you may watch lobster fishermen hauling, baiting, and resetting their traps here. Seals and dolphins are also visitors to the area, so bring binoculars.

The rocks that make up the breakwater are often slippery. Winds at high tide carry salt spray over the breakwater; in winter, the spray freezes. Watch your feet as you walk, since some of the cracks between the rocks are quite wide. You may want to scramble down the sea side of the breakwater and investigate the marine life in the pockets between the rocks. Barnacles, starfish, and periwinkles cling to the rocks. You will see seaweed rising and falling with the surge of the waves.

If you come here on one of the not-so-rare foggy days, you can easily imagine you are adrift on a calm sea. The only sound you will hear will be the horns and bells of navigational warning devices.

HIKE 21 *DUCKTRAP HARBOR AND FLATS*

General description: A walk along a small harbor and down a tidal river to Penobscot Bay.

General location: Just north of Lincolnville Beach on U.S. Highway 1 in Waldo County.

Maps: DeLorme's *The Maine Atlas and Gazetteer*, Map 14.

Degree of difficulty: Easy.

Length: There are no defined trails, so the length of hike varies according to hikers' desires and the stage of the tide.

Elevations: Sea level.

Water availability: No fresh water available.

Special attractions: At Ducktrap Harbor, an extreme low tide uncovers a huge area of sandy flats. These flats are frequented by clamdiggers, who come here for a hard-shelled clam known as a surf clam. Soft-shell clams and razor clams are also found. Sand dollars abound, as do shells from a variety of marine animals. Porpoises are frequent visitors to the waters off the mouth of the river, as are harbor seals.

Best season: Year-round, although the spring tides (when the moon is full or new) bring lower water and equinoctial tides (during the spring and fall equinox, when the sun is over the equator) bring the lowest tides of all. In order to choose the best time of day to visit the tidal flats, purchase any local newspaper and consult the tide tables therein. The *Old Farmer's Almanac* includes tide tables for Maine. These almanacs are available in most grocery stores, supermarkets, and bookstores.

For more information: Rockport-Camden-Lincolnville Chamber of Commerce, P.O. Box 919M, Camden, ME 04843 (207) 236-4404; Camden Hills State Park (207) 236-0849; or Maine Department of Conservation (207) 287-3821.

Finding the trailhead: From Lincolnville Beach, go 1 mile north on U.S. Highway 1. Go past a sign for Tanglewood 4-H Camp on the left and take the next right, just before the highway crosses a tall concrete bridge. This road leads downhill past several private homes and ends on state property on a high gravel bar. The distance from U.S. 1 to the parking area is about 1,000 feet.

The hike: Ducktrap Harbor is an undeveloped state park. Casual passers-by would not know the area was open to the public. The gravelly spit near the parking area is a great place to have a family picnic.

This is a freeform hike over sandbars and flats that are often submerged. There is no actual trail. At high tide hikers must walk on a narrow spit; at low tide the outer harbor and its dunelike sandbars beckon.

When the water is lowest, look toward the end of the gravel bar. To the left is the inner harbor through which flows the Ducktrap River. Farther left is the U.S. Highway 1 bridge. The architecture of this bridge is strikingly different from most, resembling something built by ancient Romans. The river flows past the extreme end of the gravel bar and continues through the flats into Penobscot Bay. Follow the edge of the river and wear rubber boots or old shoes, since you will get wet.

To your right, on the south side of the harbor, you may see what look like sand dunes. These sandbars are uncovered only during spring tides. Walk over to a sandbar and look for holes in the sand about the same diameter as a pencil. These are air holes made by surf clams. These large hard-shelled clams may weigh a pound each. Their adductor muscles are used by Mainers as a scallop substitute, and their "foot," the triangular muscle used for propulsion, is often ground into a marvelous clam chowder. Stand with a foot on either side of an air hole and bounce up and down. If a clam is present, a stream of water will gush out. You will see empty shells of surf clams all over the beach.

Razor clams live here, too. These clams are about 6 inches long and shaped like a straightedge razor. Their edges are extremely sharp. Pick up some of the little round lumps of sand here and you may find they are pieces of dead sand dollars. Save a few or use them to skip along the water.

After exploring the sandbar, walk back to the river and find a shallow place to cross. The opposite side of the beach has more sandbars to explore. You might want to find a dry spot on the bar where you can sit and watch for porpoises. Directly across from you are Seven Hundred Acre Island, Warren Island, and Islesboro. You will probably see the Islesboro ferry as it steams to Lincolnville Beach and back.

Follow the river back to the gravel bar, where you will find an immense bed of blue mussels. These mussels are edible, but because they live on sand they are full of tiny, worthless pearls, a hazard to your teeth. By

HIKE 21   DUCKTRAP HARBOR AND FLATS

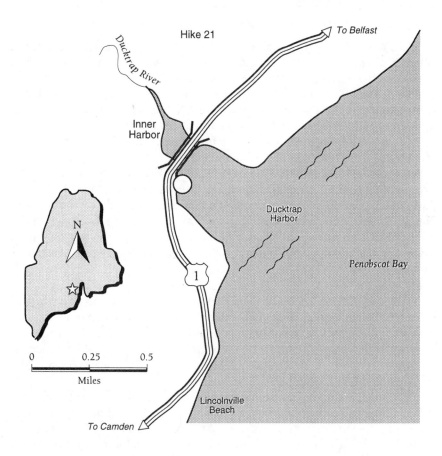

the time you are done exploring the harbor, the tide should be on its way back in, forcing you to leave whether you are ready or not.

Ducktrap Harbor is so-called because in years past giant oak trees ringed its shore. Ducks swimming in the inner harbor were easy prey, since they had difficulty gaining altitude because of the almost impenetrable ring of trees.

URBAN HIKES OVERVIEW

A hike through any of Maine's urban centers can be a rich experience. When hiking in towns and villages, be sure to give yourself enough time to soak in the atmosphere and become part of the place. Look for ornate moldings and colonnades on majestic old homes and imagine what things were like in the days of horses and wagons, when local shops sold food in bulk and the Maine waterfronts were forests of masts.

The past is ever-present in Maine towns and cities. Local architecture often dates from the Federal period and earlier. Many buildings in Maine's urban areas have stood since the days before 1820, when the state was the Province of Maine, Commonwealth of Massachusetts. Such history is particularly visible in Castine, a village that has been held by the French, Dutch, British, and Americans. Many of Castine's homes date back to the days of British occupation. History also comes alive at Skowhegan, where members of Benedict Arnold's expedition to Quebec during the American Revolution were compelled to laboriously portage their heavy wooden boats over the falls.

The population of many Maine towns increases considerably in summer. Often, quaint shops will spring up along what was once a tough waterfront. An influx of summer people from other states has renewed interest in the arts, which can be enjoyed in the form of public concerts, sidewalk art shows, storytelling sessions, and folklore programs. The summer scene in Maine's urban areas is rewarding.

The blight of urban crime has made few inroads in our state, and our town and city streets are safe places to walk at night. And no city in Maine is far from the country. Even Portland, Maine's largest city, is only minutes away from open farmland and unpolluted lakes and streams. Outdoors-oriented people can live in towns here and still hike, fish, and hunt without traveling any great distance.

HIKE 22 *BELFAST*

General description: A village walk through a historic seaside town.
General location: Belfast, in Waldo County, is at almost the geographic center of the Maine coast.
Maps: DeLorme's *The Maine Atlas and Gazetteer*, Map 14; also consult the *Belfast Area Directory*, available from the Belfast Area Chamber of Commerce, P.O. Box 58, Belfast, ME 04915; (207) 338-5900.
Degree of difficulty: Easy.
Length: 4-mile loop.

Elevations: No significant elevations encountered.

Water availability: Water is available at various sites and shops.

Special attractions: Belfast is rich in history and home to one of the few fish canneries still operating on the Maine coast. This old shipbuilding town once boasted of 11 boatyards, from which 360 ships took to the waves. The homes of sea captains are prominent features. Even if you have never seen a sea captain's home, you will instantly recognize one, since the glassed-in observation rooms called "widow's walks" are hard to miss.

The town is also one of the state's newest and most exciting arts communities.

Best season: Year-round.

For more information: Belfast Area Chamber of Commerce, P.O. Box 58, Belfast, ME 04915; (207) 338-5900.

Finding the trailhead: From Camden and points south, head north on U.S. Highway 1 to its intersection with Maine Route 3, in Belfast. Go right at the intersection, onto Main Street. Drive on Main until you pass under the traffic light, then turn left on Washington Street. Turn into the municipal parking lot, which is the trailhead.

The hike: Belfast Harbor is busy in summer, jammed with sailboats and other pleasure craft. At the same time, fishermen still moor their working boats here and ply their trade in the time-honored tradition.

From the trailhead parking lot, walk on Washington Street back to Main Street and head up Main Street Hill. Notice the Odd Fellows Building, an example of Romanesque Revival architecture, on the left. Cross the High Street intersection at the traffic light and continue up Main Street. At the intersection of Main and Church streets, you will see the old Belfast National Bank building on the left. This nearly triangular building is in the Victorian Gothic style. Turn left on Church Street, across from the Italianate post office and customs house, built around 1855.

On the right side of Church Street you will pass First Church, the tallest building in town. Built in 1818, this classic New England church has its original bell, cast by Paul Revere. Beyond the church, on the same side of the street, is the now-vacant Crosby Junior High School. The steps of this school were used in a scene from a popular movie filmed here in the 1950s.

Continuing along Church Street, you will pass a number of sea captains' houses, some with shingles of native slate and several brick chimneys. Many of these have historical markers in front, indicating dates of construction.

Church Street intersects with Northport Avenue. Turn right at Northport Avenue and head for Belfast City Park. The avenue is wide, lined with ancient maples and oaks. Some of these venerable trees dwarf even the tallest buildings. At 1.2 miles, turn left and walk the loop road at Belfast City Park. This park, founded in 1904, has a tennis court, baseball diamond, and swimming pool. The eastern end of the park is on Penobscot Bay. You can walk the shore here and, in rainy weather, picnic in the

HIKE 22 BELFAST

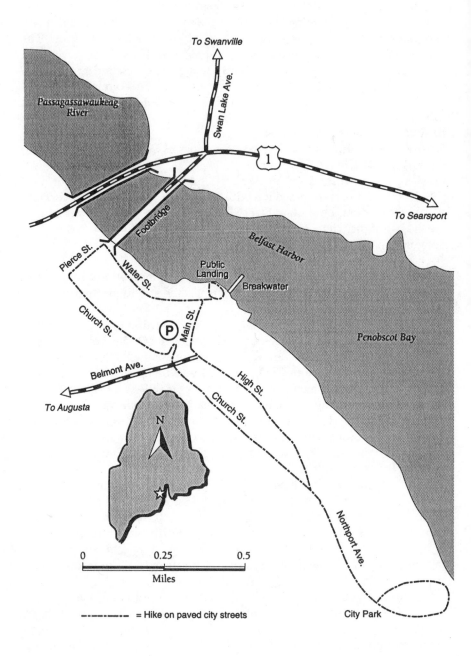

To Swanville

Swan Lake Ave.

Passagassawaukeag River

1

To Searsport

Footbridge

Pierce St.

Water St.

Belfast Harbor

Public Landing

Breakwater

Church St.

P

Main St.

Penobscot Bay

Belmont Ave.

High St.

To Augusta

Church St.

N

0   0.25   0.5

Miles

Northport Ave.

-------- = Hike on paved city streets

City Park

sheltered pavilion at the water's edge. The park is home to the Belfast Bay Festival, a major midsummer event.

Follow the park road back to Northport Avenue and turn right. Walk back toward town, and at 2.3 miles, bear right at the intersection of Church and High streets. You will walk past four different sea captains' houses. Back at the traffic light, bear right, walk to the end of Main Street, and head for the public landing at the waterfront. For a good view of the harbor, go out on the landing and to the end of the small breakwater. In summer, tour boats leave from here and take guests on rides around Penobscot Bay.

Now walk back to Main Street and turn right on Water Street. On the right are the Belfast & Moosehead Lake Railroad Station, the Old Telephone Museum, and the Railroad Theater, a year-round community theater presenting classic and modern plays. Continue down Water Street. The blue building on the right is part of Stinson Seafood Company, packers of sardines and fish steak products.

Before turning left on Pierce Street, you may want to walk out on the old footbridge. No longer used for vehicular traffic, the bridge is a swarm of activity in summer. Mackerel, bluefish, and striped bass swim under it, and local residents and tourists fish from the structure.

Walk up short but steep Pierce Street. At the intersection of Pierce and High streets, turn left. You stand across from the Governor Anderson School, a brick structure dating from 1935. Head back toward town, passing the Frick Gallery on the left and more sea captains' homes on the right. At the traffic light, turn left and return to the municipal parking lot.

Although Belfast still looks as it did 20 years ago, do not be fooled by appearances. The same structures that once housed fish markets and dry goods stores now offer paintings, crafts, and curios made by local artisans. Yet youngsters pass these same stores, rods in hand, on the way to fish from the old footbridge, just as their parents did several generations ago.

HIKE 23 *CASTINE*

General description: A walk through a historic village with eighteenth- and nineteenth-century Georgian and Federalist houses, a Revolutionary War fort, and the Maine Maritime Academy.

General location: The Castine Peninsula in Hancock County, midcoastal Maine, is bordered by Penobscot Bay on the east and the Bagaduce River on the west. Castine is nearly opposite Belfast across the bay.

Maps: A town map is available from the Castine Merchants Association, P.O. Box 329, Castine, ME 04421; see also DeLorme's *The Maine Atlas and Gazetteer*, Map 15.

Degree of difficulty: Easy.

Length: 1.7-mile loop.

HIKE 23   CASTINE

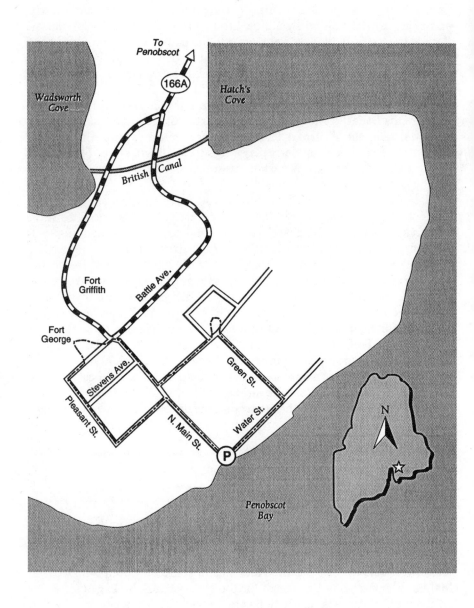

State of Maine at her berth, center photo, near the trailhead at Castine.

Elevations: No significant elevations.

Water availability: This is a village walk, so there are no springs or streams. Bring your own water.

Special attractions: Fort George State Park, Dice Head Light, Fort Madison, sea captains' houses, and other historic buildings. Historical markers give detailed information, making the tour a walk through history. Castine is home port for *The State of Maine*, the 533-foot training vessel of the Maine Maritime Academy.

Finding the trailhead: From Bucksport, take U.S. Highway 1 east to Orland and turn right on the Castine Road, also known as Maine Route 175. Follow ME 175 to West Penobscot, then go south on Maine Route 166. At the junction of ME 166 and ME 166A, bear right on ME 166A and follow the signs for Castine village. Upon reaching the peninsula, you will drive over the British Canal, built during the War of 1812. Follow ME 166 to Battle Avenue. From Battle Avenue, turn left on Main Street and park at the town landing at the bottom of the hill. This is the trailhead.

The hike: Discovered by French explorer Samuel de Champlain in 1604, the site of Castine village was occupied by Native Americans, French, Dutch, and British before becoming part of the state of Maine.

To see the town, walk uphill from the town landing and take a right on Water Street. The harbor is plainly visible on the right; on the left is a hedge fence. Turn left on Green Street, by telephone pole 10, and walk up the hill. On your left is the site of a barn used as a hospital by the British in 1815.

Directly across from the barn site is the Fort George Bank, built in 1814 and moved to this location in 1818.

Green Street intersects Court Street. Directly opposite you at the left-hand corner of the town square is the Witherle Memorial Library, where a courthouse and jail stood in the 1790s. Walk out on the square and stand in front of the Civil War Soldier's Monument. On your right, you will see the Unitarian Church, built in 1790. The church has a steeple designed by Charles Bulfinch, who designed the U.S. Capitol, and a genuine Paul Revere bell.

Turn about and face Court Street. Go right on Court; you will see Emerson Hall on your left. Dedicated in 1901, Emerson Hall serves as town hall and office building. Now go right on Main Street. On the left is the 1829 Trinitarian Church. At the top of the hill are the brick buildings of the Maine Maritime Academy on the left. You now face Battle Avenue. Cross the street and walk up to Fort George, built in 1779 and now a state park. The fort is the site of the first hanging in Hancock County. On a summer night, residents assert they can hear the ghost of the drummer boy beating the dead march.

Go back to Battle Avenue and turn left on Pleasant Street. On your right a sign indicates the campground of the Hamilton Regiment, a British unit that attacked and captured the American Halfmoon Battery in 1779. Walk down Pleasant Street, where you will see magnificent oak and elm trees on either side of the road. Just past the soccer field, take a left on Court Street and pass a sea captain's home dating from the 1820s. Turn right on Main Street and head downhill to the town landing, where you started.

HIKE 24 *ROCKPORT VILLAGE*

General description: A village walk beginning in an old limestone quarry, going up a short main street, through a public garden, and down a country road above Penobscot Bay.
General location: In Rockport just south of Camden in Knox County, midcoastal Maine.
Degree of difficulty: Easy.
Length: 3-mile loop.
Elevations: Slight.
Water availability: None, except at stores and restaurants.
Special attractions: Rockport is off the beaten path and surpasses more popular towns in beauty and historical significance. Several lime kilns preserved here are examples of a once-thriving industry. A granite statue of Andre the seal, the unofficial town mascot, can be seen at the town landing. The Children's Chapel is a beautifully landscaped garden spot overlooking Penobscot Bay. It is a favorite location for weddings.

HIKE 24 ROCKPORT VILLAGE

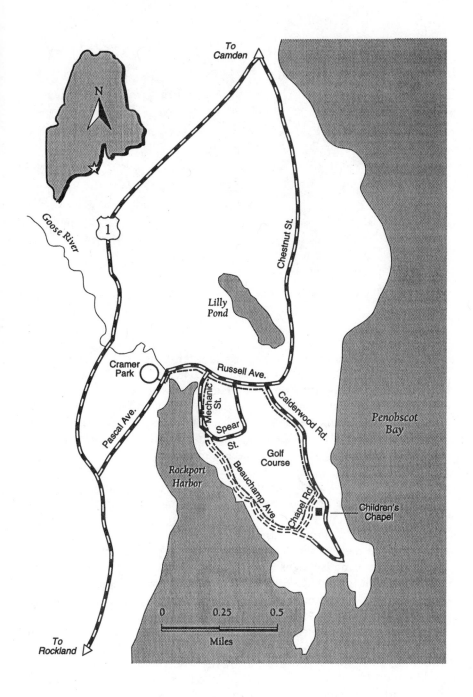

Steps at Children's Chapel.

Best season: Year-round.
For more information: Rockport-Camden-Lincolnville Chamber of Commerce, P.O. Box 919M, Camden, ME 04843; (207) 236-4404.
Finding the trailhead: From Camden, head south on U.S. Highway 1. Just past Libby Chevrolet on the right, turn left on Pascal Avenue. Go straight down Pascal Avenue for 4 miles until you see Rockport Harbor on the right. On the left, you will see a sign for Cramer Park. Drive in to the Cramer Park parking area. This is the trailhead.

The hike: Cramer Park is the site of an abandoned limestone quarry. The limestone you see around here is the same material you would use to sweeten garden soil. The size of the crater here gives you an idea of the extent of mining activities in the area.

From the park, walk out to the main road, past several observation points and informative signs. Cross the highway bridge over Goose River and bear right, up a hill. You are now in Rockport village. Many of the buildings are made of native granite and brick. Several benches offer you a chance to pause and take in the surroundings.

Go past the Rockport Opera House, on the right. This is next to Mary Lea Park, a small but pretty resting place. Bear right past and walk down the main road. Now you are out of the village center and in a quiet residential district. Continue straight to a fork at 0.8 mile, and take the right-hand lane, which is Calderwood Road.

Walk past a golf course on both sides of the road. Go straight. The road becomes narrow, lined with stately cedars. Bear right on Chapel Road and at the fork take the left-hand street to the Children's Chapel. The chapel itself sits on a high ledge and is surrounded by a host of perennial plants and ornamental shrubs. From here you can look out and see sailboats on Penobscot Bay.

Return to the fork on Chapel Road and go down the right-hand lane. This is an unpaved road lined on both sides by huge cedars. At 1.5 miles you will come to a stop sign. Take the road to the right. (This section is sometimes closed to vehicular traffic from December until spring.) Pass a farm, where you may be greeted by two burros by the roadside. On the left, you can now see Rockport Harbor.

This road is a country lane within the village. Magnificent oaks line the road on your right; you can watch activity in the harbor on your left. The road goes downhill here, with several winding curves. At 2 miles, you will see a granite ledge projecting out into the harbor. You may want to walk down to it.

Now the road goes slightly uphill. On the right is a striated granite ledge, and on the right the land slopes down to the water. At 2.2 miles, the road turns to pavement. Walk uphill to a stop sign at the corner of Spear and Mechanic streets. Turn left on Mechanic Street. From this point, you can look to the north and see the craggy top of Mount Battie, in Camden. Continue up Mechanic Street to another stop sign. Turn left here and head back to the village, by crossing the bridge.

Before heading back to Cramer Park, take a left and walk down to the town landing. Here you can inspect the lime kilns, see the statue of Andre, the famous seal (subject of a recent movie), sit on a bench, and watch the goings-on in this busy little harbor. Return to Cramer Park.

HIKE 25   *SKOWHEGAN*

General description: A village hike beginning on the banks of the Kennebec River near a Revolutionary War historic site, passing through a city park, and ending at a dam on the river.
General location: About 15 miles northwest of Waterville, in Somerset County, central Maine.
Maps: DeLorme's *The Maine Atlas and Gazetteer*, Map 21.
Degree of difficulty: Easy.
Length: 4.4 miles round-trip.
Elevations: No significant elevations encountered.
Water availability: Water is available at several locations.
Special attractions: Hikers may see more than 200 species of shrubs, trees, and flowers along the Kennebec River in 12.5-acre Coburn Park, a riverside picnic area. Various entertainers perform here on Sunday

HIKE 25 SKOWHEGAN

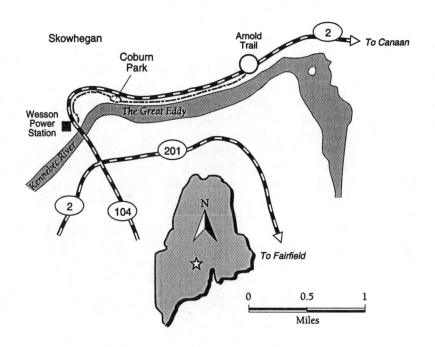

afternoons in the summer.

Best season: May through October is most enjoyable.

For more information: Skowhegan Chamber of Commerce, Municipal Parking Lot, Skowhegan, Maine 04976; (207) 474-3621.

Finding the trailhead: From points south, go north on Interstate 95 through Waterville and get off at Exit 36. Take U.S. Highway 201 north to Hinckley, and turn right on Maine Route 23. Cross the Kennebec River at Pishon Ferry and proceed north to the junction of U.S. Highway 2, in Canaan. Turn left on U.S. 2 and continue to Skowhegan, where you will see a sign for the Kennebec Banks Rest Area on the left, alongside the river at a place called the Great Eddy. Park at Kennebec Banks. This is the trailhead.

The hike: Abnaki Indians named the local falls Skowhegan, which loosely translated means "a place for watching." These same falls, which now power Central Maine Power's Wesson Power Station, presented the men of Benedict Arnold's expedition to Quebec with a formidable challenge. Their heavy wooden bateaus had to be laboriously hauled up and around them.

The hike begins at Kennebec Banks. Walk west along U.S. 2, which follows the Kennebec River. The river is wide here with a strong, steady current. If you come here in late spring, you will probably see numbers of brown trout breaking the water as they gobble up mayflies and other aquatic insects.

At a little over 1 mile, the road goes slightly uphill. Watch for the turnoff to Coburn Park on the right. The park was a gift to the public from Governor Abner Coburn more than 100 years ago. It is situated on a bluff overlooking the Kennebec River. Walk through the park and stop by the fence at the back of the park. From here, you can look directly down on the turbulent waters of the river, which is divided by an island at this point.

Continue walking to town, where you will pass the church of Notre Dame De Lourdes on your right. This is a magnificent stone building, much like a cathedral from the Middle Ages. From here, walk on to a bridge over the river. On the left, steps lead down to an observation point where you can get a bird's-eye view of Wesson Powerhouse and the falls.

Leave the observation point and at 2.2 miles cross the bridge over the Kennebec River. From here, as you look downstream, try to imagine how Arnold's men felt as they pulled their heavy boats up and over this natural impediment. Follow the same route back to the trailhead.

High water on Kennebec River. Site of Arnold Expedition route.

HIKE 26 *PORTLAND TRAILS*

General description: A hike along Baxter Boulevard in Portland, going completely around Back Cove, a nearly round cove of Casco Bay.
General location: The City of Portland in Cumberland County on Maine's South Coast.
Maps: "Linking Open Spaces, A Vision For Portland Trails," is available from Portland Trails, One India St., Portland, ME 04101. Call Alix Hopkins at (207) 775-2411; see also DeLorme's *The Maine Atlas and Gazetteer*, Maps 3 and 5.
Degree of difficulty: Easy.
Length: 3.75-mile loop.
Elevations: Sea level.
Water availability: Bring your own water.
Special attractions: The Back Cove Trail represents a pleasant diversion for a visitor to the city. The route takes you completely around a sheltered inlet. Shorebirds abound here, offering a unique chance to watch and photograph wildlife in an urban setting.
Best season: Year-round.
For more information: Portland Trails, One India St., Portland, ME 04101; (207)-775-2411. You may also write to the Friends of the Parks

Along Back Cove at low tide.

HIKE 26 PORTLAND TRAILS

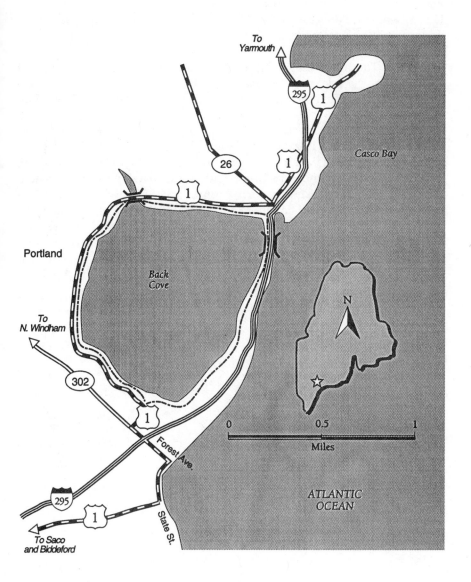

Commission, c/o Portland Department of Parks and Public Works, 55 Portland Street, Portland, ME 04101.

Finding the trailhead: From points south, take U.S. Highway 1 to Portland and turn left on Forest Avenue. From here, take a right again on U.S. 1, which follows the perimeter of Back Cove. Parking is available at various points along the trail.

The hike: The trail winds completely around Back Cove. Depending on the height of the tide, the cove may be full of water or the mudflats may be exposed. Only that section of the cove near the entrance to Casco Bay is deep water.

Back Cove Trail is actually one small part of a larger vision. Portland Trails, a nonprofit organization, is dedicated to creating a 30-mile network of recreational trails within Greater Portland by 1996. Current projects include several trails: the **Fore River Trail**, a 3-mile trail within the 85-acre Fore River Sanctuary; The **Eastern Promenade Shoreway Trail**, a 1.5-mile abandoned railroad corridor at the base of the Eastern Promenade projecting into Casco Bay; the 1.5-mile **Capsic Pond Trail**; the **Stroudwater River Trail**; and the **Baxter Trail**, which links Back Cove with Evergreen Cemetery. Work has already begun on the Eastern Promenade Trail, and the barrier-free trail will be completed in 1996.

The Back Cove Trail is accessible to people in wheelchairs.

CAMDEN HILLS HIKES OVERVIEW

When a guest on a Boston radio show was asked what her plans were for the summer, she said that she would be teaching music in Camden, Maine. The show's host replied with tongue in cheek, "That's tough work, but somebody has to do it."

Camden is a fine place to spend a season. An oceanside town where mountains meet the coast, it is a haven for hikers and artists. The bird's-eye view of the village and its snug harbor, as seen from the summit of Mount Battie, appears on postcards and placemats found all over New England.

Hikers can see this panorama as well as fine inland views from the mountain summits of the Camden Hills. The hills have often been referred to as "the other Acadia," with good reason. Camden Hills State Park offers camping within the shadow of Mount Battie and strolls along Penobscot Bay. It can serve as home base for hikers interested in exploring some or all of the varied geography of the region. The area's hikes rival those of Acadia with their spectacular scenery—and, happily, few hikers take advantage of them,

HIKE 27   *MOUNT BATTIE AND MOUNT MEGUNTICOOK*

General description: A day hike to two mountain summits with panoramic views from an ocean lookout.
General location: Near the village of Camden in Knox County, midcoastal Maine.
Maps: The Appalachian Mountain Club's *Maine Mountain Guide* map of the Camden Hills and DeLorme's *The Maine Atlas and Gazetteer*, Map 14; a map of the trails in Camden Hills State Park is supplied at the park entrance.
Degree of difficulty: Moderate. The Mount Battie Trail is steep and rocky and can be difficult when wet or icy.
Length: 4 miles round-trip.
Elevations: Mount Megunticook, the highest of the Camden Hills, is 1,385 feet.
Water availability: No reliable water on the trail, so bring your own.
Best season: April through November.
For more information: Camden Hills State Park, Camden, ME 04843; Bureau of Parks and Recreation, Maine Department of Conservation, State House Station 22, Augusta, ME 04333; (207) 289-3821.
Finding the trailhead: From Camden and U.S. Highway 1, take Maine

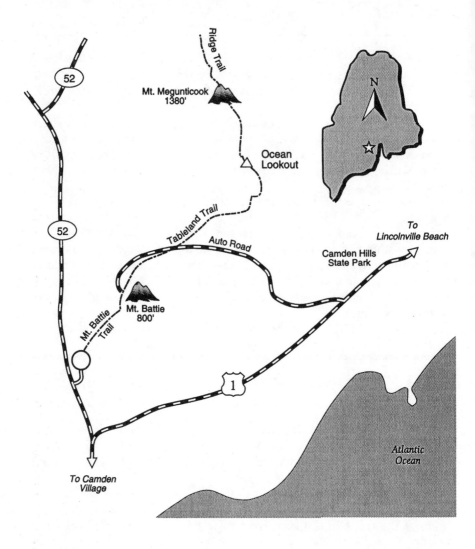

Route 52 northwest. Take the first right, Megunticook Street; follow this street to its end. At the top of what looks like a private driveway is a small parking area. The white-blazed Mount Battie Trail begins here.

In good weather you might consider parking in town, since the extra walk to the parking area is no more than a mile. This would be a good idea if you plan to hike the alternate route back, going by way of Camden Hills State Park.

The hike: Follow the white blazes for a 0.5-mile hike to the first mountain summit on the **Mount Battie Trail**, which is very steep and rocky. Limited views can be had at selected ledges a few minutes up the trail. At the summit is a stone tower commemorating those who fought in World War I.

Continue following the blazes across the parking area and into the forest. This is the **Tableland Trail**. On it you will soon cross a road and begin climbing Mount Megunticook through a hardwood forest of red oaks and beeches. This forest has been designated part of the Maine Critical Areas Program.

At the junction of the Tableland Trail and the **Mount Megunticook Trail**, coming up from Camden Hills State Park on U.S. Highway 1, is **Ocean Lookout**. This lookout offers fine views of the hills to the west, Mount Battie, the village of Camden, and Penobscot Bay.

The **Ridge Trail** begins here as a continuation of the Tableland Trail. This takes you to the wooded summit of Mount Megunticook. Return by the same trails or, alternately, take the Mount Megunticook Trail down to the state park and walk back to Camden. For a longer hike, you can take the **Scenic Trail** to the **Maiden Cliff Trail** and back.

HIKE 28   *BALD ROCK MOUNTAIN*

General description: A day hike to the summit of a mountain overlooking the upper reaches of Penobscot Bay.

General location: Camden Hills State Park west of Lincolnville Beach and north of Camden in Knox and Waldo Counties, midcoast Maine.

Maps: The Appalachian Mountain Club's *Maine Mountain Guide* has a map of the Camden Hills; see also DeLorme's *The Maine Atlas and Gazetteer*, Map 14; and maps of trails in Camden Hills State Park are available at the park entrance.

Degree of difficulty: Easy to moderate. The final leg of the trail leading to the summit is steep, but offers no technical difficulties.

Length: 3.6 miles round-trip.

Elevations: The Bald Rock summit is at 1,100 feet.

Water availability: No reliable water on the trail, although the Ski Shelter Trail crosses a seasonal brook.

Special attractions: The view from the summit is spectacular, and the trail is never crowded. In winter, the Ski Shelter Trail is used for cross-country skiing. A shelter near the summit is suitable for an overnight stay. Check with park officials before planning an overnight trip.

Best season: Year-round.

For more information: Camden Hills State Park, Camden, ME 04843; Bureau of Parks and Recreation, Maine Department of Conservation, State House Station 22, Augusta, ME 04333; (207) 289-3821.

Finding the trailhead: From Camden or Lincolnville Beach take U.S. Highway 1 to Maine Route 173 west. Go 3 miles on ME 173 and turn left at its junction with Youngtown Road. A parking area and a large

HIKE 28 BALD ROCK MOUNTAIN

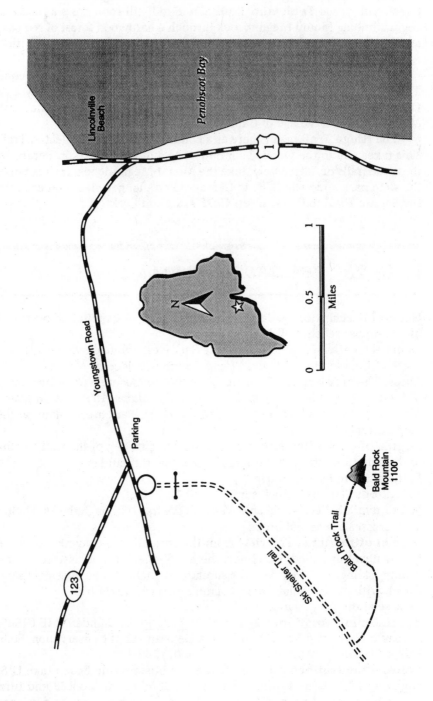

Heading back to the trailhead on Ski Shelter Trail.

wooden hiking trail sign are on the immediate left. The trail begins at the parking lot.

The hike: The **Ski Shelter Trail** was once drivable but has deteriorated to the point that park officials have put up a steel gate to prohibit vehicular traffic. Walking up the trail is easy at first, but the path becomes steeper as you proceed. Pace yourself here, since the **Bald Rock Trail**, which you will encounter later, is quite steep and will require energy.

As you walk, you will notice that the woods turn from a mix of hardwoods and evergreens with a few ancient apple trees to mostly evergreens. The spruces are pleasingly pungent here; you can detect this perfume of the north woods almost as soon as you begin the trail. You may find a quantity of spruce gum, the resin that flows when the bark of a tree is damaged and hardens upon contact with air. Brittle at first, the gum gains a true chewing-gum texture when moistened.

After hiking 1.3 miles up the Ski Shelter Trail you will come to a grove of mature white pines on the left. A sign here indicates a distance of 0.5 mile to the summit via the Bald Rock Trail. The Bald Rock Trail gets steep in a hurry. Fortunately, several sets of granite steps have been installed, making for easy climbing. The trail goes through a series of switchbacks. After what seems like more than 0.5 mile, you will see open sky through the evergreen canopy. The summit is near.

The summit offers outstanding views of Islesboro, Lincolnville Beach, and Deer Isle, on the other side of Penobscot Bay. The ferryboat going between Islesboro and the mainland looks like a child's toy from here.

View to the southeast from Bald Rock summit.

Grassy areas on the summit have patches of Labrador tea, a low shrub used as a substitute for Oriental tea during the American Revolution.

Return to the parking lot by the same trails. Another trail traces a steep route to U.S. 1 from the eastern side of the summit. To make use of this trail, you should have another vehicle parked on U.S. 1 to take you back to the trailhead.

HIKE 29 RAGGED MOUNTAIN

General description: A hike up a ski slope to a summit with good views of the Maine interior and the Atlantic Ocean.
General location: Southwest of Camden in Knox County, midcoast Maine.
Maps: The Appalachian Mountain Club's *Maine Mountain Guide* has a map of the Camden Hills; see also DeLorme's *The Maine Atlas and Gazetteer*, Map 14.
Degree of difficulty: Easy.
Length: 2.2 miles round-trip.
Elevations: The summit is 1,300 feet above sea level.
Water availability: No water on trail.
Special attractions: A view of the Camden Hills from the southwest, which gives a different perspective on the region.

Best season: April through October.

For more information: Camden Snow Bowl Ski Area, Hosmer Pond, Camden, ME 04843; (207) 236-3438.

Finding the trailhead: From Camden, go south on U.S. Highway 1 and turn right on John Street. Follow the signs to Snow Bowl Ski Area and park in the parking area by Hosmer Pond. The hike begins at the metal gate in front of the ski area.

The hike: Follow the chairlift up the grassy ski slope. In summer, this is a wildflower meadow, with black-eyed Susans, hairy vetch, daisies, yarrow, and wild strawberries.

Before reaching the end of the chairlift, walk to your right through one of the breaks in the strip of woods separating the chairlift from the T-bar. Walk to the top of the T-bar and follow a rocky path that goes under a power line. Take the wooded trail on your immediate right. This trail is marked with orange flagging.

The trail loops around to the southwest and winds through a narrow cleft, where the trail forks. The main trail continues toward South Hope, as indicated by a sign. The trail to the summit and its radio tower is on the left. A short walk through rocky blueberry land leads you to the top.

Views from the summit include Maiden Cliff, Bald Mountain, Mount Megunticook, Camden, and the Atlantic Ocean, as well as inland Maine, to the west. Return to the top of the ski slope by the same trail, then hike down to the parking area by following either lift.

Ragged Mountain view to the southwest.

HIKE 29 RAGGED MOUNTAIN

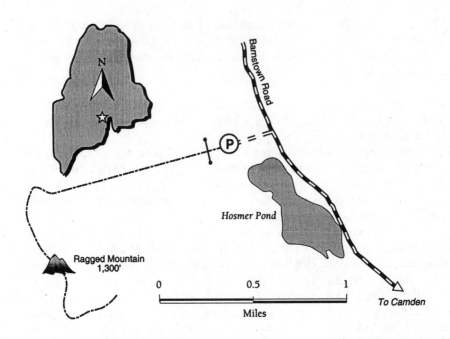

HIKE 30   *MAIDEN CLIFF*

General description: A hike to a rocky outcropping above Megunticook Lake, featuring spectacular inland views.

General location: About 3 miles west of Camden in Knox County, midcoast Maine.

Maps: The Appalachian Mountain Club's *Maine Mountain Guide*; DeLorme's *The Maine Atlas and Gazetteer*, Map 14.

Degree of difficulty: Easy.

Length: 1.8 miles round-trip.

Elevations: Maiden Cliff rises 800 feet.

Water availability: The trail crosses a seasonal brook.

Special attractions: Can be combined with other trails in Camden Hills State Park to make a full day of hiking. Camera buffs will like this trail: The views of Megunticook Lake and surrounding countryside give outstanding opportunities for photographs, especially in autumn.

Best season: April through November.

HIKE 30 MAIDEN CLIFF

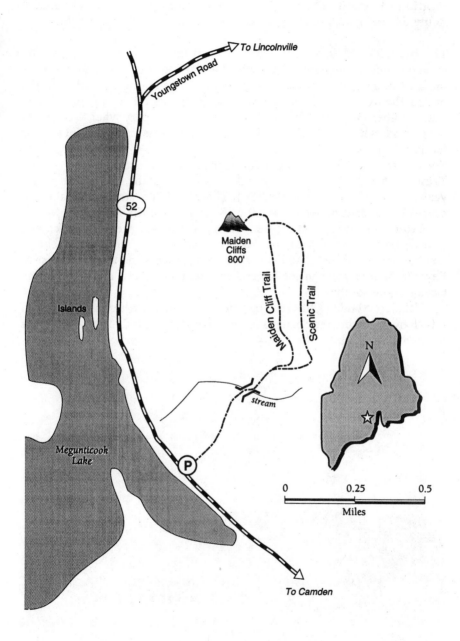

For more information: Camden Hills State Park, Camden ME 04843; Bureau of Parks and Recreation, Maine Department of Conservation, State House Station 22, Augusta, ME 04333; (207) 289-3821.

Finding the trailhead: From Camden and U.S. Highway 1, take Maine Route 52 and go 2.9 miles to an elevated parking area on the right.

The hike: The Maiden Cliff Trail begins at the north end of the parking lot and winds through mixed growth. The trail bears northeast and follows the bank of a small brook before crossing a wooden bridge. Shortly past the bridge, the **Ridge Trail** meets the Maiden Cliff Trail. Keep to the left. The trail becomes quite steep here. The rocks can be slippery when wet, as can the ground itself, since it has a blanket of pine needles, so be careful of your footing.

The trail follows the ridge and just past the junction of the **Scenic Trail,** ends at Maiden Cliff. A wooden cross marks the spot where an 11-year-old girl fell to her death in 1864. That should be enough to make you proceed with caution when walking about on the cliffs.

From the lookout at Maiden Cliff you can see Megunticook Lake directly below. Looking into the lake, you can identify underwater shoals just below the surface: The deepest areas are where the water is darkest. Beyond the lake you can see Ragged and Bald mountains and the Atlantic Ocean to the south.

Take the Maiden Cliff Trail back to the trailhead. Alternately, you can return by following the Scenic Trail to the Ridge Trail, then go back to the Maiden Cliff Trail.

Maiden Cliff with Megunticook Lake in foreground.

DOWNEAST HIKES OVERVIEW

The term "Downeast" is a holdover from the days of sailing ships and refers to the way ships took advantage of prevailing winds to head in a given direction. Downeast Maine is northeast of the midcoast area, although no hard and fast boundaries exist. (People from the midcoast and south coastal regions often claim to be Downeasters.) Washington and Hancock counties make up its undisputed bulk.

Downeast Maine is vast country. Its mountaintops offer 100-mile vistas and sweeping pictures of New Brunswick, Canada, on the other side of Passamaquoddy and Cobscook bays. Distances here are huge, so hikers interested in bushwhacking through the region need to be thoroughly prepared for a long haul. The climate is similar to that of midcoast Maine, except that the average temperatures are a few degrees cooler, so hikers should dress accordingly.

If a contest were held to name the last real frontier in the east, Downeast Maine would be a top contender. Here fishermen ply their trade as their ancestors have done for centuries, and people can still live unfettered lives in a truly rural environment. The Downeast area is still largely wild and is home to the few remaining wild Atlantic salmon runs in America. It also has a large black bear population.

HIKE 31   BLACK MOUNTAIN

General description: A steep climb to the summit of a mountain on public reserve land with good views of surrounding lakes and mountains.
General location: The Tunk Lake region of Downeast Maine northeast of Ellsworth in Hancock County.
Maps: DeLorme's *The Maine Atlas and Gazetteer*, Map 24.
Degree of difficulty: Moderate. Although the trail is steep, it is well kept.
Length: 2.2 miles round-trip.
Elevations: 1,094 at the highest summit.
Water availability: Bring your own water.
Special attractions: Black Mountain is surrounded by lakes and ponds and is near several other mountain trails. A hiker could spend several days in this area, walking over varied terrain.

Cairns and stone steps mark this trail. Atop the mountain, cairn builders have waxed poetic. Monoliths set among miniature spruces remind visitors of a Japanese garden.
Best season: Late April through October.
For more information: USDA Forest Service, Cherryfield, ME 04622; (207) 546-2346.

HIKE 31   BLACK MOUNTAIN

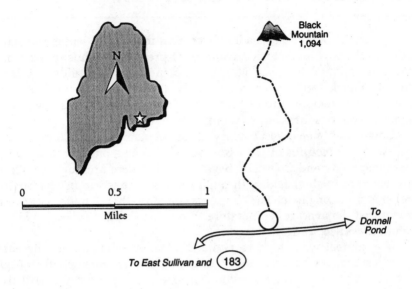

Finding the trailhead: From Ellsworth, head east on U.S. Highway 1, also known as the Star Memorial Highway. Turn left on Maine Route 183, known as the Tunk Lake Road. Go up ME 183 for about 4.5 miles, where you will cross an abandoned railroad track. Take the next left on Fire Road 34K, about 400 feet past the tracks. This is a dirt road with a good surface. The Black Mountain trailhead is 2.5 miles up this road. Be sure to go straight on this road, avoiding the few turnoffs. The road becomes less traveled but is still passable for any two-wheel-drive vehicle. The trailhead is marked by small cairns of stones on both sides of the road and a few bits of flagging on the left.

The hike: The trail winds uphill from the beginning through a dense spruce forest. You will pass large numbers of granite boulders. The trail is well-marked with cairns and pink flagging. It quickly breaks into an oak forest where rocks are covered with moss. The forest floor is studded with boulders here. The only way you know you are on the trail is to follow the cairns, which are numerous.

At 0.3 mile, the rocks thin out and the trail bears to the left through more oaks. Steps in the trail are made of native granite. At 0.4 mile, you will see a solid granite ledge looming above. You can explore this ledge and others in the vicinity, but don't do this if the rocky floor is wet, since you could lose your footing. You can walk under ledge overhangs in any

Below the ledge at Black Mountain.

weather, examining various mosses and lichens that live on the rocks. Huge, square blocks of granite have sheared off from the main body and fallen away. Yellow flags lead you through this boulder field.

After the ledges, the trail bears sharply left. You leave the oak woods as the trail winds steeply through a spruce forest. Many years' worth of spruce needles pad the trail, making for soft footing.

At 0.6 mile, the trail is steep and goes over the stark faces of granite ledges. Fragrant bayberry and low-growing juniper can be found beside the rocks. At 0.7 mile, you reach the first mountaintop, where other hikers have fashioned a primitive rock garden.

In order to reach the higher summit, take the trail past Wizard Pond, a narrow trail to the right. This trail is variously marked with cairns and pink flagging. The trail winds near the top of a promontory, then bears uphill and to the left. At 0.8 mile, cairn builders have made a stone arrow to indicate the direction of the trail.

At 1 mile, you will come to a precipice and several deeply fissured ledges. Follow the trail for another 0.1 mile to the true summit.

Hikers may wish to try several nearby hikes in the same day. If you only go 0.3 mile up Fire Road 34K and go left, rather than straight, you will come to the Donnell Pond-Schoodic Beach parking area. Here you will see wooden trail signs leading to the top of Schoodic Mountain, as well as a new trail to Black Mountain.

HIKE 32   *SCHOODIC MOUNTAIN*

General description: A hike to the summit of a mountain northeast of Frenchman Bay.

General location: Near the town of Sullivan about halfway between Ellsworth and Cherryfield in the Tunk Lake region, Hancock County.

Maps: DeLorme's *The Maine Atlas and Gazetteer*, Map 24.

Degree of difficulty: Mostly easy, with 0.75 mile of moderately difficult trail.

Length: 5.5 miles.

Elevations: The summit is 1,069 feet above sea level.

Water availability: The trail crosses a reliable stream at 0.5 mile. At the time of this writing, the water was safe for drinking.

Special attractions: Offering a panoramic view of the mountains of Acadia National Park, this hike is a good way to get your legs in shape after a long winter.

Best season: May through November.

For more information: Appalachian Mountain Club's *Maine Mountain Guide*; DeLorme's *The Maine Atlas and Gazetteer*.

Finding the trailhead: From Ellsworth, drive east on U.S. Highway 1 to the town of Sullivan. From Sullivan, take Maine Route 200 north to East Franklin, where you will see a pullout between two bridges. This is the trailhead.

The hike: This is a popular hike, so if you go on a weekend in summer you will probably see other hikers. The trail begins on a paved road leading east from the trailhead. At 0.1 mile, the trail heads left on a dirt fire road. You have a good view of Schoodic Mountain from this point.

At 0.5 mile, the trail crosses a small brook.

At 1 mile, the trail crosses some railroad tracks, follows them to the right for a short distance, then turns left and into mixed woods of white pines, oaks, and maples. For the next 0.5 mile, the trail is intersected by several forks. Stay to the left at each fork.

At 1.9 miles, the trail bears left at an intersection with another forest road. Go left. A short distance up the trail look for an unmarked but well-worn trail that leads uphill to an old foundation, the site of a fire warden's camp. The trail leads to the left of the foundation and gets quite steep, going over open ledges. The views get better as you climb. Here and there a cairn indicates the direction, as do lengths of old telephone wire.

At the summit, a radio tower has taken the place of the old fire tower. Since the summit is open and flat, you can walk around and enjoy views in every direction. To the south are the mountains of Acadia, to the east are Black and Catherine mountains, and to the north is Lead Mountain.

Return to the trailhead by the same route.

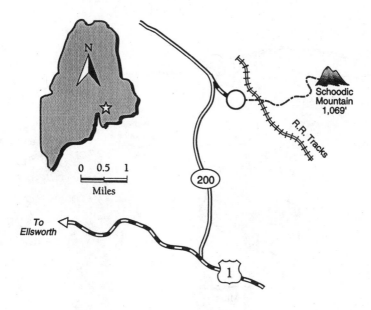

HIKE 33   *CATHERINE MOUNTAIN*

General description: A day trip to a mountain summit.
General location: Northwest of Franklin and Tunk Lake in Hancock County. The mountain is bordered on the west by public reserve land.
Maps: DeLorme's *The Maine Atlas and Gazetteer*, Map 24.
Degree of difficulty: Easy.
Length: 1.4 miles round-trip.
Elevations: 942 feet at the summit.
Water availability: No water on trail.
Special attractions: Old slag piles at the top are evidence of past mining activities. Local rumor says that the soft metal mined here was used during wartime as a hardening agent for gunmetal.
Best season: Late April through October.
For more information: USDA Forest Service, Cherryfield, ME 04622; (207) 546-2346.
Finding the trailhead: From Franklin, head east on Maine Route 182. Go past Fox Pond on the right of the road. Just past the pond, drive up a hill and look for a turnout on the right. Park here and look for a narrow road heading into the woods. Although the road looks drivable, it soon becomes impassable. You must walk in from here.

HIKE 33 CATHERINE MOUNTAIN

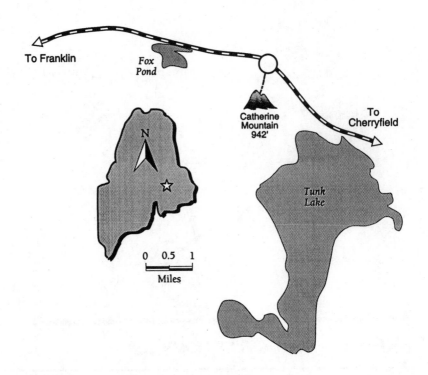

The hike: Follow this dirt road until it becomes a trail. Some blue flagging may be seen, if crows and ravens haven't carried it away. Go another 0.5 mile to the summit, where you will see slag piles and a series of ledges.

The ledges on top of the mountain beckon hikers to leave the trail and do a bit of exploring.

HIKE 34 *PEAKED MOUNTAIN*

General description: A hike on an old forest road and up a steep trail to the rocky summit of a mountain.
General location: East of Brewer near the town of Clifton, Penobscot County, Downeast Maine.
Maps: DeLorme's *The Maine Atlas and Gazetteer*, Maps 23 and 24.
Degree of difficulty: Easy to moderate. The steep section is quite short, making this a generally easy hike.
Length: 2.6 miles round-trip.
Elevations: The summit is 1,160 feet above sea level.

Water availability: A small stream behind the site of the old warden's cabin is usually flowing, but the quality is questionable.

Special attractions: The exposed granite face of Peaked Mountain, also known as Chick Hill, is visible for miles around. The views from the summit are some of the best in the area.

Best season: Year-round. The hike can be done on snowshoes if you take special care to stay well away from precipices.

For more information: Consult DeLorme's *The Maine Atlas and Gazetteer* or the Appalachian Mountain Club's *Maine Mountain Guide.*

Finding the trailhead: From Brewer, go east on Maine Route 9, also known as the Airline, to East Eddington. Continue through East Eddington and look for the intersection with Maine Route 180, on the right. This is Clifton Corners. Continue on ME 9 for 3.5 miles and look for the campground at Parks Pond on the right. Turn north across from the campground. The pavement ends soon. After 0.6 mile, you will come to a graveled parking area. Be sure to park well to the side, because this is a turnaround for the local school bus. The parking area is the trailhead.

The hike: Walk straight up the hill directly across from the parking area. The trail is steep and rocky at first, but at 0.2 mile it becomes easier.

HIKE 34   PEAKED MOUNTAIN

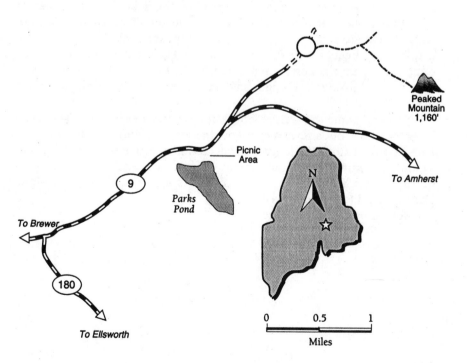

Looking down at Little Chick Hill from Peaked Mountain.

A small stream flows by on your left, behind the site of an old warden's cabin.

At 0.5 mile, there is a cabled tote road on the right. Soon after that you will come to another road branching off to the left. Turn right here onto a narrow road marked by old blazes. The trail passes through a stand of oaks, maples, and beeches. At 0.8 mile, another trail comes in from the left. Continue to bear right on the main trail. At 0.9 mile, the trail climbs steeply up a rugged hillside. You might have to use small trees to pull yourself up here.

You will come to exposed ledges at approximately 1 mile. The trail is indistinct here, but a few cairns show the way. Behind you is Little Chick Hill. Continue along the ledges, and at 1.3 miles you will reach the Peaked Mountain summit and a panoramic view of the Penobscot River to the north, Mount Katahdin to the northwest, and the mountains of Mount Desert Island to the southeast.

Return by the same route.

HIKE 35 *DEDHAM BALD MOUNTAIN*

General description: A hike up a lone mountain to an abandoned fire tower and superb views.
General location: Northeast of Bucksport near Dedham in Hancock County.
Maps: DeLorme's *The Maine Atlas and Gazetteer*, Map 23.
Degree of difficulty: Steep, but otherwise easy.
Length: 1.4 miles round-trip.
Elevations: The summit is 1,234 feet above sea level.
Water availability: No water available.
Special attractions: Dedham Bald Mountain is not as popular as some of the more well-known peaks in Maine, probably because it is off the beaten path. The quality of the hike and the views from the summit make this one of the better day trips in Downeast Maine. As of 1994, the fire tower at the summit was safe to climb. The tower offers some of the best views around.
Best season: March through November.
For more information: Maine Forest Service, (206) 287-2775.
Finding the trailhead: From Bucksport, take Maine Route 46 north. After 2 miles, take the first right. At Mast Hill Road, turn left and head north again. Just across from a small pond on the left, turn right on North Orland Road. Go about 2 miles on this road to Dedham Road. Go north (left) on Dedham Road to the trailhead at the parking area at the base of the mountain on a sharp curve in the road. The parking area is the trailhead.

The hike: From the parking area, walk straight up an easily identified trail. What appears to be a fork in the trail is only an offshoot and comes back to the main trail after a short distance. Continue on the main trail, which becomes quite steep. The trail goes over a granite ledge, demanding careful walking. Lowbush blueberries line the trail on both sides. As you climb, the view becomes increasingly better, since the entire trail is open and exposed.

The summit is quite flat, allowing you to walk about and check out views in different directions. The best views are from the fire tower, however. From here, on a clear day, you can see Mount Katahdin, Bigelow Mountain, the city of Bangor, Phillips Lake, and Green Lake to the north, and the mountains of Acadia National Park to the east.

The fire tower at the summit of Dedham Bald Mountain.

HIKE 35 DEDHAM BALD MOUNTAIN

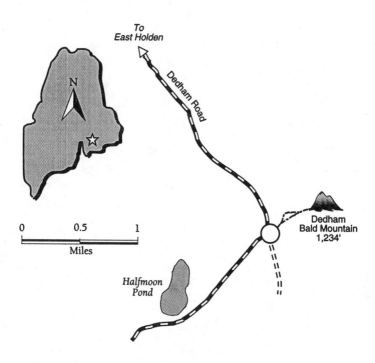

To
East Holden

N

Dedham Road

0   0.5   1
Miles

Halfmoon
Pond

Dedham
Bald Mountain
1,234'

HIKE 36 *REVERSING FALLS PARK*

General description: A hike on a peninsula that goes through fields, woodlands, and by a narrow channel where the tide moves fast enough to cause a low waterfall to reverse itself.

General location: East of Dennysville and south of the town of Pembroke in Washington County on a peninsula in Cobscook Bay.

Maps: The Triangle Grocery on U.S. Highway 1 in Pembroke has handmade maps available to the public; see also DeLorme's *The Maine Atlas and Gazetteer*, Maps 27 and 37.

Degree of difficulty: Easy.

Length: 0.8 mile loop.

Elevations: No significant elevations encountered.

Water availability: No water available.

Special attractions: This municipal park is located on a remote point of land where the tide moves so fast that a person running cannot keep up with it. This park is one of the best spots to observe the terrific height and force of the Bay of Fundy tides. Islands and ledges offer good photo

HIKE 36 REVERSING FALLS PARK

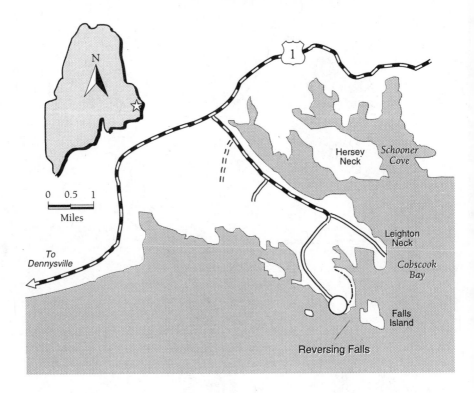

opportunities. Ospreys and bald eagles glide over the bay and look for fish.
Best season: April through November.
For more information: Consult DeLorme's *The Maine Atlas and Gazetteer.*
Finding the trailhead: From Dennysville, head north on U.S. Highway
1 and turn right at the Triangle Grocery in Pembroke. Drive a short
distance and turn right by the Odd Fellows Hall and follow Leighton Neck
Road. Watch for the intersections of unmarked roads on the right, and turn
right on the third road, which was recently resurfaced. After the turn, you
will pass a cemetery on the right. Drive down a steep hill. At the head of
a small cove turn left. Continue on this road to where it turns to gravel.
After 6.1 miles, you will come to a turnaround at Reversing Falls Park. This
is the trailhead.

The hike: This is a short hike, but you could spend a whole day here
exploring the woods and coast at your leisure. From the trailhead, head
down a path to the right. Pass a fenced-off family burial ground, dating
from the mid-nineteenth century. The trail takes you through an open side
hill with a few spruce trees and down to the shore. Bear left and follow the
trail by the water's edge to Reversing Falls. Or bear right and hike the shore

Reversing Falls Park. The dark horizontal line indicates tidal zone.

on your own; you can go for a considerable distance.

Continue down the trail, following the shore. You can walk out on ledges at almost any place. As you near the falls, the roar of the rushing water becomes more pronounced. An island only 100 yards out in the channel causes a huge rip. If the tide is out, you can clearly see the high-tide mark on the reddish granite of the island and the ledges on the other side of the channel.

Standing opposite the falls, you hear the noise and sheer power of the current is hard to believe. Crosscurrents cause random whirlpools. Ospreys are common, idly riding the air currents. If you are not in a hurry, you might want to spend some time here just sitting and watching the grand spectacle.

From the falls, the trail rounds a point and follows a narrow, protected cove. Several lobster boats sit grounded at the head of the cove. From here, at 0.4 mile, the trail bears left and heads up to the field. (You also can continue along the cove, past the lobster boats, and follow the trail into the woods for a short distance, then backtrack to the trail.) On the way back to the field, the trail is covered with a network of spruce roots. At the field, follow the gravel road to the trailhead, at 0.8 mile.

A side trip to the end of the peninsula is worth taking. To get there, continue straight on Leighton Neck Road on the way in and drive to its end on a wide, secluded beach. Vehicles drive up and down the entirely unrestricted beach on both sides. There are no signs here, no parking fees, and no lifeguards—only the pristine waters of Cobscook Bay, the constant wind, and a few sea birds.

General description: A structured hike on trails in a wildlife refuge through upland terrain.

General location: Between Calais and Woodland in northern Washington County.

Maps: A map of Moosehorn National Wildlife Refuge is available at the refuge or from the U.S. Fish and Wildlife Service, 300 Westgate Center Drive, Hadley, MA 01035; (413) 253-8200. See also DeLorme's *The Maine Atlas and Gazetteer*, Map 36.

Degree of difficulty: Easy.

Length: 1.9 miles on various trails.

Elevations: No significant elevations encountered.

Water availability: Bring your own water.

Special attractions: Moosehorn is the only refuge in the nation specifically managed for American woodcocks. The Woodcock Trail, a descriptive nature walk recommended for those who are physically challenged, shows the detailed management techniques employed in studying these birds. Visitors are invited to participate in woodcock and waterfowl banding operations. Check the schedules ahead of time to coordinate your trip with a banding operation. Moosehorn also is home to nesting bald eagles, which

Red pines along the Nature Trail, Moosehorn National Wildlife Refuge.

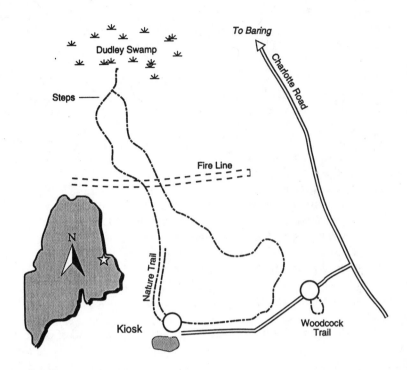

can be observed at Magurrewock Marsh or around Dennys Bay.

The 50 miles of roads and trails at Moosehorn are closed to motor vehicles but open to hikers, skiers, and snowmobilers. Fishermen may try the streams and ponds at the refuge. A boat landing is provided at Bearce Lake, and there is a barrier-free fishing access at the Baring unit.

Best season: Year-round, but spring and fall are the best times to observe most wildlife species.

For more information: Visit refuge headquarters on Charlotte Road at the Baring Unit, or contact the Refuge Manager, Moosehorn National Wildlife Refuge, P.O. Box 1077, Calais, ME 04619; (207) 454-7161.

Finding the trailhead: From Calais, take U.S. Highway 1 west for 3.5 miles. Look for a sign indicating the refuge on the left, just past the Magurrewock Marsh. Turn here on Charlotte Road. You will come to the refuge headquarters in 3 miles. On the way, you will pass the trailhead for the Woodcock Trail; the headquarters parking lot is the trailhead for the Nature Trail.

The hike: Moosehorn National Wildlife Refuge consists of the Baring (16,080 acres) and Edmunds (6,665 acres) units. Between the two units, 7,460 acres have been set aside as wilderness areas.

The hike consists of two different trails near the headquarters. After turning onto Charlotte Road, you will see a sign on the left indicating the beginning of the **Woodcock Trail**. Park here and take the path to the right of the parking area. This trail is barrier-free in its entirety; a leaflet describes six different sites along the trail. This is a highly instructive, educational hike for anyone interested in the habits and management of the American woodcock. The trail loops, returning to the parking lot at 0.4 mile.

Next, walk or drive to refuge headquarters. A kiosk at the parking lot contains maps, leaflets, and exhibits describing the refuge. Pick up a trail map for the **Nature Trail**. A sign behind the kiosk marks the beginning of the trail.

The trail goes under a power line, with spruce trees on the right and pines on the left. The first stop along the trail is between a mowed field on the right and a partially grown-up field on the left.

The trail swings to the left and enters a monoculture of white pine. At 0.2 mile, you come to a giant wolf pine, the largest pine on the refuge. The trail bears slightly downhill by the edge of a field and leaves the pine stand, going into a mixture of hardwoods and softwoods.

At 0.4 mile, the trail begins to loop back toward the headquarters, going uphill. The trail passes through a stand of large red pines. At Stop 4 you can witness the power of a black bear's teeth. The bear was attracted by the salt content of the paint, and the sign is left to show you what the teeth marks look like.

The trail goes through more mixed growth, then a stand of poplars, and at 0.5 mile winds over a ridge where you can see a considerable distance through the woods. At 0.6 mile, you come to an intersection. Go right and walk through a monoculture of red pine. The trail crosses a fire line made to prevent forest fires from spreading. On the other side of the fire line, the trail enters a stand of white pine and heads downhill. At 0.8 mile, you have a choice: You can go uphill and back to the headquarters, or you can go straight on to the **Marsh Loop**.

The Marsh Loop is actually a spur trail that takes you to the edge of Dudley Swamp. The wooden box here, resembling a birdhouse, is a wood duck nesting box. Such boxes are responsible for restoring wood duck numbers to their present healthy levels.

Walk back to the woods and take the trail to the right, where you will encounter a steep bank with wooden steps. At 1 mile, you will come to a clearing that was created for woodcocks to use for courtship rituals. At 1.2 miles you will cross the fire lane again and enter a large, open piney woods. At 1.3 miles you will enter a forestry cut, the last stop on the Nature Trail. From here, the trail becomes a gravel road and takes you back to the headquarters at 1.5 miles.

On the way back to U.S. Highway 1, look for the observation shelter/ blind and handicapped fishing access off Charlotte Road Park on the right side of the road and follow a surfaced path to a wooden structure projecting over a stream. This shelter has a roof and slots on both ends for observing wildlife in complete comfort. The far end of the structure provides access for fishermen.

HIKE 38   *QUODDY HEAD STATE PARK*

General description: A hike along the top of a spectacular seaside bluff at the easternmost point of the United States.
General location: Just south of Lubec in Washington County across Lubec Channel from Campobello Island, New Brunswick, Canada.
Maps: DeLorme's *The Maine Atlas and Gazetteer*, Map 27.
Degree of difficulty: Mostly easy with a few steep areas.
Length: 1.4 mile loop.
Elevations: The bluffs rise 200 feet above the water.
Water availability: Bring your own water.
Special attractions: The Bay of Fundy has the strongest tides in the world. Tidal variations here can run as high as 26 feet. The red-and-white striped West Quoddy Head Lighthouse is a historic landmark, built in 1807 and rebuilt in 1852. You can walk down to the lighthouse, only a short distance from the trailhead. Grand Manan Island, Canada, is plainly seen across the bay.
Best season: May through November.
For more information: The Bureau of Parks and Recreation, Maine Department of Conservation, State House Station 22, Augusta, ME 04333; (207) 287-3821.
Finding the trailhead: From U.S. Highway 1 in Whiting, head east on

West Quoddy Head State Park.

111

HIKE 38 QUODDY HEAD STATE PARK

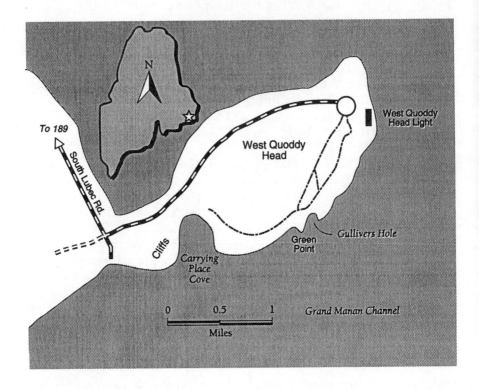

Maine Route 189 by a sign for Quoddy Head State Park. Go 9.7 miles on ME 189 toward Lubec and turn right by a Texaco gas station at the intersection of South Lubec Road. Follow this road to the parking area at West Quoddy Head.

The hike: The parking area is only open in summer. If you come here in spring or fall, park just outside the gate within sight of the lighthouse. The gate marks the trailhead.

Walk in past the gate and at 0.2 mile bear left at the parking lot. Look for a path on the ocean side of the lot and walk to the right on this path. The trail follows the shoreline. From here, you can look to the left and see the lighthouse; to the right you can see the bluff. At 0.4 mile the trail winds up the head. This is a steep climb, with rocks and waves directly beneath you. The trail follows the very edge of the cliffs with a steep hill coming down from the opposite side, leaving you nowhere to go but straight ahead.

At 0.6 mile, you come to Gulliver's Hole, a sea cave directly below you. Wire cables prevent you from scrambling down for a closer look. From Gulliver's Hole, the trail becomes steep. Ladderlike steps have been placed here to assist your passage. As you walk up High Ledge, listen for a dull roar, the result of air being forced through a crack at the base of the cliffs.

The best time to hear this is at high tide, but it can be present at any stage of the tide.

From High Ledge, at 0.7 mile, turn around and follow your steps back to a fork. Bear left on the inland trail, which takes you through an extremely thick grove of fir trees. Follow this path back to the trailhead.

HIKE 39 SHORE TRAIL

General description: A hike on an isolated peninsula through one of the few stands of jack pine in the state.

General location: The Petit Manan National Wildlife Refuge on Petit Manan Point near Milbridge in Washington County.

Maps: Maps of the trail are shown on wooden signs at the trailhead; see also DeLorme's *The Maine Atlas and Gazetteer*, Maps 17 and 25.

Degree of difficulty: Easy for the most part, but if you choose to hike the shore, the rocks make for hazardous walking.

Length: 2.4 miles round-trip.

Elevations: No significant elevations encountered.

Water availability: None.

Special attractions: This hike takes place in an isolated coastal area. Few people other than locals are aware of this trail. You can enjoy the rugged Maine coast in peace and tranquillity here.

Best season: April through December.

For more information: Petit Manan National Wildlife Refuge, P.O. Box 279, Milbridge, ME 04658; (207) 546-2124.

Finding the trailhead: From Milbridge, take U.S. Highway 1 a few miles west. Look for Pigeon Hill Road directly across from the Rusty Anchor Restaurant. Turn and follow Pigeon Hill Road for 6.2 miles to a gravel parking area. This is the trailhead.

The hike: Leave your vehicle at the parking lot and walk south on the gravel road for 0.5 mile until you see a sign indicating the **Shore Trail**. Here also see a wooden trail sign with a map.

From the sign, walk through a field with lowbush blueberries. At the end of the field, enter a woodland, where another sign indicates the trail. An interpretive sign here tells a bit of the natural history of white-tailed deer. Deer tracks can be seen on an obvious deer trail that crosses the path here.

Enter the woods and cross a little wooden bridge over a wet area. Walk up a rocky hill through stunted spruces. The trail goes across a granite ledge. The woods are mostly low scrub bushes, with some beech and larch trees. At 0.8 mile, you come to a fork with a sign pointing to the left. Turn here, and you get your first peek at the ocean.

HIKE 39 SHORE TRAIL

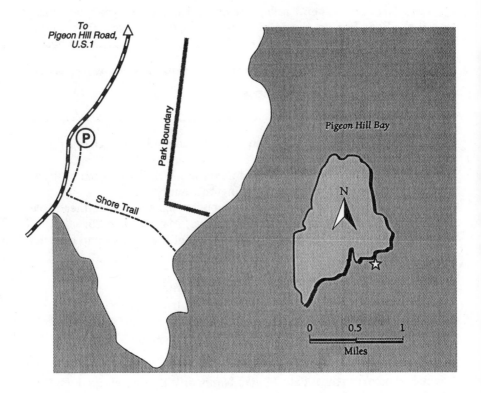

Go up a barren hill with blueberry bushes and stunted cedars. The trail bears slightly to the right and goes through a large stand of jack pines. Some of these pines are growing at crazy angles, giving the appearance of Bonsai trees. At 1 mile, you come to a granite ledge, where you may need to use your hands to lower yourself. After the ledge, see a sign which tells about the jack pines. These trees are colonizers, building soil for other trees. They shed cones that only open in the heat of a forest fire.

Now you are almost down to the water. Cross a rough-hewn bridge over a wet area, just past the jack pines. A sign near the water's edge reminds you that this is not a loop trail. At 1.2 miles, walk down to the beach. Notice the wave-washed, smooth stones. You can walk out on a rough ledge and get a good view of the ocean and Bois Bubert Island across the channel.

Return to the trailhead the way you came in. Or follow the shoreline south across more rock ledges and pebble beaches before returning.

General description: A hike through upland woods and along several ocean coves.
General location: Just off U.S. Highway 1 near Whiting in Washington County.
Maps: DeLorme's *The Maine Atlas and Gazetteer*, Map 27.
Degree of difficulty: Easy.
Length: 2.1-mile loop.
Elevations: No significant elevations encountered.
Water availability: If you come in spring or fall, bring your own water.
Special attractions: One particular attraction at this park is the clamming. In most parts of Maine, you must have a permit to dig clams—if the clamflats are even open. But here you can dig up to 1 peck of soft-shelled clams per person. If you camp at the park, you will probably want to experience the thrill of digging your own clams and steaming them at your campsite.
Best season: April through November.
For more information: Cobscook Bay State Park, P.O. Box 51, Dennysville, ME 04628; Bureau of Parks and Recreation, Maine Department of Conservation, State House Station 22, Augusta, ME 04333; (207) 289-3821.
Finding the trailhead: From Whiting, take U.S. Highway 1 north and watch for a sign on the right indicating Cobscook Bay State Park. Turn right here. Go 0.4 mile and look for a large sign on the right. Drive in on a tarred road and park to the right of the registration station. The trailhead is marked by a rather obscure sign to the right of the parking area.

The hike: Except in high summer, you probably won't see any other hikers here. The **Nature Trail** takes you through a truly wild, wooded area and along a sheltered cove.

Walk into the woods by a sign for the Nature Trail. The trail is marked with blue blazes. At 0.2 mile, the trail goes slightly downhill, through an old clearing. Young fir dominates the area as the pioneer species here. Look to the right of the clearing and you will see an impenetrable fir thicket. I saw black bear scat on the trail here.

At 0.4 mile, go down a little gully. The trail takes a sharp left by the site of a long-gone bridge across a small stream. The trail becomes narrow, winding through a dense fir thicket, then climbs steeply up an eroded bank. At the top is a rope for you to grab for support.

The trail now becomes indistinct, but the blue blazes show you where to head. At 0.6 mile, the stream becomes larger, and the trail heads inland. You get your first look at the Whiting Bay from here. At 0.8 mile, go down a bank and cross a wooden bridge. After crossing the bridge, come to an intersection by a sign pointing to campsite 105. Follow this trail to the right

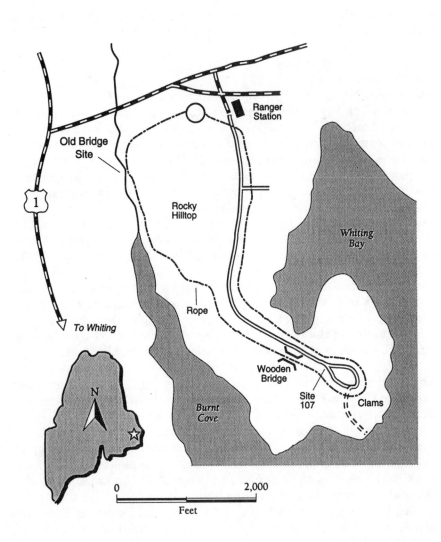

Ranger
Station

Old Bridge
Site

1

Rocky
Hilltop

Whiting
Bay

Rope

To Whiting

Wooden
Bridge

Site
107

Clams

N

Burnt
Cove

0   2,000

Feet

through a cedar grove. On the left, see a rocky hilltop. At 1.2 miles, walk up to a picnic table and shelter overlooking the bay. You can see campsite 107. Turn right here and go down to a protected harbor. A sign points out the daily limit for clams. Walk back to campsite 107 and at 1.3 miles take the camp road back to the trailhead. You can see the bay to the right as you head slightly uphill. At 1.6 miles, a spur trail leads to the top of the rocky hilltop mentioned earlier. At 2.1 miles, you are back where you started.

HIKE 41   *BIRDSACRE SANCTUARY*

General description: Several trails and ponds in a woodland sanctuary.
General location: Southeast Ellsworth in Hancock County.
Maps: DeLorme's *The Maine Atlas and Gazetteer*, Map 24.
Degree of difficulty: Easy.
Length: 2-mile loop.
Elevations: No substantial elevations encountered.
Water availability: An open spring along the trail looks inviting, but the possibility of contamination is too risky. Bring your own water.
Special attractions: This hike is a must for families with children. In addition to hiking, you can visit the Stanwood Homestead Museum, once the home of Cordelia J. Stanwood, an ornithologist, photographer, and

The Queen's Throne in Birdsacre Sanctuary.

HIKE 41 BIRDSACRE SANCTUARY

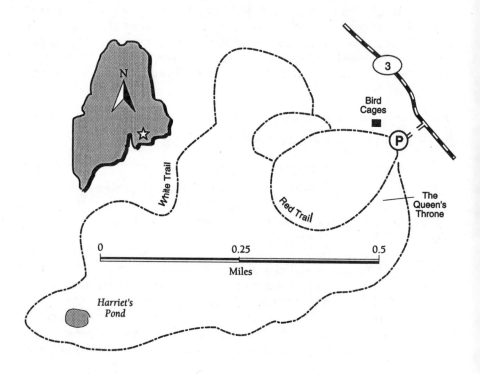

author. You can look at caged birds, including various hawks and owls, part of the sanctuary's wildlife recovery center. Birdsacre does not charge for parking or using the trails.

Best season: May through October.

For more information: Call (207) 667-8460.

Finding the trailhead: In Ellsworth, turn right at the traffic light by Dunkin' Donuts and head east on Maine Route 3. After about 2 miles, on the right you will see a sign for Birdsacre Sanctuary. A small building at the edge of the parking lot gives a history of Birdsacre as well as information about Cordelia J. Stanwood. A trail sign to the right of the information building marks the trailhead.

The hike: For those headed for Acadia National Park from the south or west, Birdsacre is a welcome break from urban sprawl. Although the entrance is on busy U.S. Highway 1, all signs of suburbia vanish when you enter the parking lot.

The wooden hiking trail sign at the trailhead is too complex to memorize. Numbers of lesser trails crisscross from one side of the main trail to the other. If you wish to spend much time exploring the different trails, you should carry a notebook and make a working map.

Two main trails, the **White Trail** and the **Red Trail**, form the back-bone of the trail system. The longest is the White Trail, at 2 miles. The trail is easy to follow because of white blazes on trees and trail signs at regular intervals. If you didn't make a rough map to carry with you, be sure to stick to the marked trail. Do not be fooled by a sign pointing to the perimeter trail, since it leads to a dead end.

The White Trail leads through mixed growth forest. In June, sheep laurel, pink lady's slippers, Indian paintbrush, and daisies bloom along the trail. You should have ample chance to study or photograph these plants from the rough benches placed regularly along the trail.

Halfway around the trail, a clearing beckons you to tarry a bit. This is the site of Harriet's Pond. Sit down on a bench, listen to the bird songs, and watch dragonflies chasing mosquitoes.

As you near the end of the trail, you will see a giant boulder called the Queen's Throne. A large white pine has incorporated this boulder into its trunk, forming an ersatz lounge chair.

The White Trail ends at the parking lot.

HIKE 42 CROCKETT COVE WOODS

General description: A hike through a foggy, dense forest of spruce and fir in a preserve held by The Nature Conservancy.
General location: Deer Isle, a relatively unspoiled island between East Penobscot Bay and Jericho Bay in Hancock County.
Maps: DeLorme's *The Maine Atlas and Gazetteer*, Map 15.
Degree of difficulty: Easy.
Length: Nature Trail and Loop Trail, 0.25 mile; Orange Trail, 1 mile.
Elevations: No significant elevations encountered.
Water availability: No water available.
Special attractions: The drive to Deer Isle is an enjoyable trip by itself. As you leave the mainland, cross the Deer Isle-Sedgwick Bridge, a high, narrow suspension bridge built in 1939. A causeway brings you to Deer Isle. The roads here are mostly narrow and winding with little sign of commercialism. Most of the residents still make their living from the sea in one way or another.

The hike takes place in a fog forest, a damp but beautiful place where mosses and lichens cover rocks, trees, and the trail itself. The focal point is the Nature Trail, a self-guided interpretive hike.
Best season: Year-round, but summer and fall are best.
For more information: Maine Chapter, The Nature Conservancy, Fort Andross, 14 Main Street, Suite 401, Brunswick, ME 04011; (207) 729-5181.
Finding the trailhead: From U.S. Highway 1 in East Orland, take Maine Route 15 south to Deer Isle. Watch for a right turn to Sunset at Deer Isle village. Turn right on Whitman Road, about 3 miles from the Sunset post

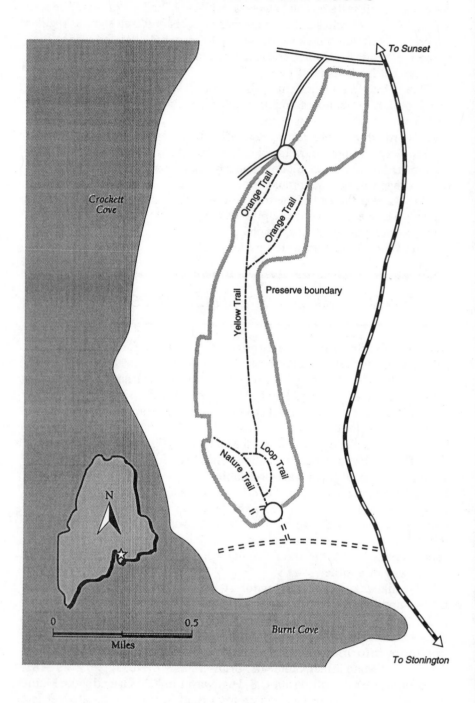

To Sunset

Crockett
Cove

Orange Trail

Orange Trail

Yellow Trail

Preserve boundary

Loop Trail

Nature Trail

N

0   0.5

Miles

Burnt Cove

To Stonington

office. Watch for Fire Lane 88 on your right. Follow the fire lane to a small parking lot and registration box.

The hike: Walk straight in from the parking area. The spruce and fir woods here are quiet, except for the distant sounds of navigational devices in the bay.

On the right, a spruce tree grows out of a fissure in a mossy granite ledge. Continuing down the path, you come to the beginning of the **Loop Trail** on the right. Take the **Nature Trail**, which goes downhill from here. At the bottom of the hill on the right, you will see a large nub strewn with huge granite boulders. The boulders are covered with various mosses, the predominate variety being Schreber's moss. Striped maple, an understory tree, grows here as well.

Pass a huge boulder on the right. This is a glacial erratic deposited around 12,000 years ago. At the other end of the Loop Trail continue straight on spruce planks laid over a boggy area where sphagnum moss and carnivorous pitcher plants grow. Soon you come to the preserve boundary. Turn around here and head back to the Loop Trail, which is now on the left.

The Loop Trail goes up the nub and over granite boulders. This is a short but steep climb. Footing can be tricky, since the trail is covered with spruce needles. The serpentine trail winds through the spruces and mossy boulders until you arrive back at the parking lot. Be sure to sign at the registration box if you haven't already done so.

As a second hike, you might want to walk the **Orange Trail**. Drive back to Whitman Road and head north. Turn left on Fire Lane 96. Proceed down the fire lane to another small parking area and registration box. The Orange Trail is a narrow, 1-mile trail winding through a dense spruce forest.

HIKE 43   *PINEO RIDGE*

General description: An unstructured walk on a glacial plain, featuring wave-washed rocks and kettle hole ponds.
General location: Near Columbia Falls and Cherryfield in Washington County.
Maps: DeLorme's *The Maine Atlas and Gazetteer*, Map 25.
Degree of difficulty: Easy.
Length: Pineo Ridge is crisscrossed with miles of gravel roads and paths. Hikers can decide how far to go and how long to stay.
Elevations: No significant elevations.
Water availability: No water available.
Special attractions: Pineo Ridge is one of the best examples of glacial topography in the eastern United States. This area is one vast plain with kettle holes. The ridge is used for lowbush blueberry cultivation. Although

HIKE 43   PINEO RIDGE

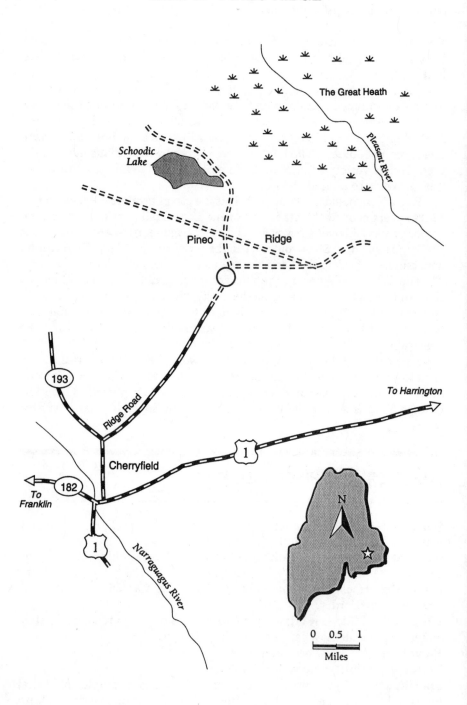

The barrens, depression to left of center is a kettle hole.

natural vegetation is scarce, blueberry growers have planted windrows of pine trees to help reduce erosion.

Best season: Mid-April to May 1 and July through October. Honeybees are brought to Pineo Ridge to pollinate blueberry blossoms and are usually active through May and June. Swarming bees can be dangerous, so do not come during bee season.

For more information: Consult DeLorme's *The Maine Atlas and Gazetteer*.

Finding the trailhead: From the south on U.S. Highway 1, cross the Narraguagus River in Cherryfield. Just past the bridge, take the first left and head north on Maine Route 193. At about 1.5 miles, take the surfaced road to the right. Continue on this road for about 5 miles. Here you will see a sign on the left warning about the danger of honeybees during May and June. Shortly after passing the sign, take a left turn at a fork. Here you will see a pile of irrigation pipes. Park off the road. This is the trailhead.

The hike: As you hike, be careful not to go off the paths, since blueberry plants are fragile and subject to damage.

Look for a gravel road to your right. Walk down this road for about 0.1 mile and you will see kettle holes on both sides. The kettle holes, so common here, were formed when a glacier melted, leaving enormous blocks of ice. As the land sprang back up, relieved of the weight of the mile-thick ice, these blocks kept certain areas below the median ground level. When these last blocks melted, kettle holes reamained.

Go back to the main road and look for an intersection, just ahead. This is the Baseline Road, about 5 miles long. This road is used as a control point for most of the large land surveys in the east. You can walk the length of this road.

From here, the main road bears left and circles Schoodic Lake. Paths and lesser roads bear off in both directions. Pull off the road and walk any of these to get a feel for the vastness of the barrens. Beware of fog, though; people have been lost in the fog while wandering these primitive roads.

Northeast of Pineo Ridge is the Great Heath, the largest raised bog in Maine. The Pleasant River traverses the heath, and you can put a canoe in at several points and explore it that way. It is a great spot for birding and viewing bog plants. Much of the heath is on public reserve land. To get there, go another 0.5 mile up the surfaced road you drove in on and look for another gravel road to the left. This takes you to the Pleasant River. Consult DeLorme's *The Maine Atlas and Gazetteer* for more information.

SOUTH COAST HIKES OVERVIEW

The south coast region contains the bulk of Maine's population, although the country remains delightfully rural. Portland, Maine's largest city, is located along the south coast only a few scant miles from unspoiled countryside.

The grasslands and sand beaches of the region are home to grasshopper sparrows, piping plovers, and least terns, all endangered species. Certain trees can be found growing naturally only in this part of the state—Atlantic white-cedars, shagbark hickories, sweet birches, American chestnuts, and sassafras.

Hikers will find that south coast Maine is the warmest section of the state, which makes it a good place to visit in cooler months. Flowers bloom on the south coast while ice and snow still blanket inland areas.

HIKE 44 *JOSEPHINE NEWMAN SANCTUARY*

General description: A hike in an Audubon sanctuary around a rugged, wooded peninsula bounded by salt water.

General location: Located on Georgetown Island, a remarkably pristine island southeast of Woolwich in Sagadahoc County.

Maps: DeLorme's *The Maine Atlas and Gazetteer*, Maps 6 and 7.

Degree of difficulty: Easy to moderate. Some sections of the trail are steep, but none present any particular difficulty.

Length: 1.8 miles on various trails.

Elevations: No significant elevations encountered.

Water availability: No water available.

Special attractions: Recommended for those who long for a private, unfettered experience with nature. This sanctuary is one of the more charming and little-used hiking areas in the state. An unsung treasure, it is never crowded and always rewarding.

Best season: April through November.

For more information: Maine Audubon Society, 118 U.S. Highway 1 (Route 1), Gilsland Farm, Falmouth, ME 04015; (207) 781-2330. The Maine Audubon Society can provide you with a publication about Newman Sanctuary.

Finding the trailhead: From U.S. Highway 1 in Woolwich, take Maine Route 127 south. Go 9 miles, until you reach the U.S. Post Office in Georgetown. Cross a bridge just past the post office and look for an inconspicuous, unpaved road on the right. This road enters ME 127 at such an acute angle that you may have to drive past, turn around, and enter from

HIKE 44 JOSEPHINE NEWMAN SANCTUARY

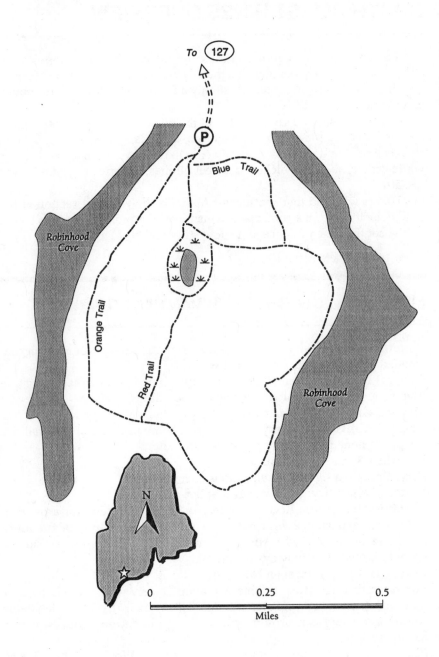

the opposite direction. A small sign announces the Josephine Newman Sanctuary. Drive slowly down the dirt road and park in a small parking area. A sign shows a map of the trails.

The hike: From the parking area, walk down a cabled-off path to a kiosk and trail map on the edge of a field. From the kiosk, walk to the right, on the **Orange Trail**. Orange trail markers adorn wooden posts at irregular intervals. Looking to the right, you catch glimpses of Robinhood Cove.

At the end of the field, a marker indicates the path into the woods. Small pines, all the same size, make you think that this might have been pasture at one time. Pass some spreading oaks and ground juniper. Orange metal triangles indicate the trail. At 0.3 mile, the trail takes you to a little bluff overlooking the water.

Go slightly uphill through a grove of small oaks. At 0.5 mile, you can see a steep gully to the right. The trail goes uphill and becomes slightly steeper. By a stone fence, the trail forks. Go left. The trail follows the stone fence by some striped maples, also called moose maples. Now the trail crosses the fence and goes uphill by a large spreading oak and into a magnificent oak forest.

At 0.6 mile, come to the intersection of the **Yellow Trail** and the **Red Trail**. Go right on the Red Trail. The trail goes to the top of a hill, where the Red Trail turns left. At the bottom of the hill, the trail is narrow as it winds through a fir thicket. The ground is damp, covered with sphagnum moss. Sunlight cannot penetrate here because of the thickness of the firs.

At 0.8 mile, the trail is narrow, winding through thick woods, and it reaches another stone fence. Go steeply uphill and make an abrupt left, where you can look down on the salt water. Lots of spreading oaks stand here. Now the trail makes a steep descent, going nearly straight down to the water, perhaps 150 feet.

The trail now dives into the woods and makes another steep downhill. At 1 mile, the trail takes a sharp right under a giant double pine. You have arrived at marsh grass on the edge of Robinhood Cove. Smell the tang of the salt air, as opposed to the resinous odor of the upland area. You can see private homes on the other side of the cove. The trail follows the shoreline and passes large spruces and hemlocks. At the bottom of the hill you can look up at the hemlocks.

The trail goes over a rocky prominence. Be careful here; if you lose your footing, you will likely wind up in the water below. Huge lichen-covered boulders line the trail, hemming you in. At 1.4 miles, the trail becomes more tame, and at 1.6 miles you reach its intersection with the **Blue Trail**. Go straight on the Red Trail, past a small cattail-filled pond on the left. At 1.7 miles, the trail intersects with the Blue Trail once again, and at 1.8 miles, you walk back to the field with the kiosk through a break in the stone fence.

HIKE 45 *WOLFE'S NECK WOODS STATE PARK*

General description: A hike through a variety of forest types and along the rocky shores of Casco Bay.
General location: On Wolf Neck near Freeport in Cumberland County. Wolf Neck is a peninsula bounded by Casco Bay and the Harraseeket River.
Maps: A pamphlet is available at the park or from the Bureau of Parks and Recreation; see also DeLorme's *The Maine Atlas and Gazetteer*, Map 6.
Degree of difficulty: Easy.
Length: 1.6-mile loop.
Elevations: No significant elevations encountered.
Water availability: Water is available at the park.
Special attractions: In addition to the roughly 5 miles of trails described here, Wolfe's Neck Woods State Park offers self-guided nature tours, regular nature programs with a park naturalist, a 0.5-mile-barrier-free path, a picnic area, and a chance to view ospreys in the wild. This park is recommended for physically-challenged individuals, families with children, and anyone interested in learning more about the natural history of south coast Maine.
Best season: Park is open Memorial Day through Labor Day. Visitors are welcome during daylight hours year-round.
For more information: Bureau of Parks and Recreation, Maine Department of Conservation, State House Station 22, Augusta, ME 04333; (207) 287-3821.

Hiker on the Casco Bay Trail, Wolfe's Neck Woods State Park.

HIKE 45 WOLFE'S NECK WOODS STATE PARK

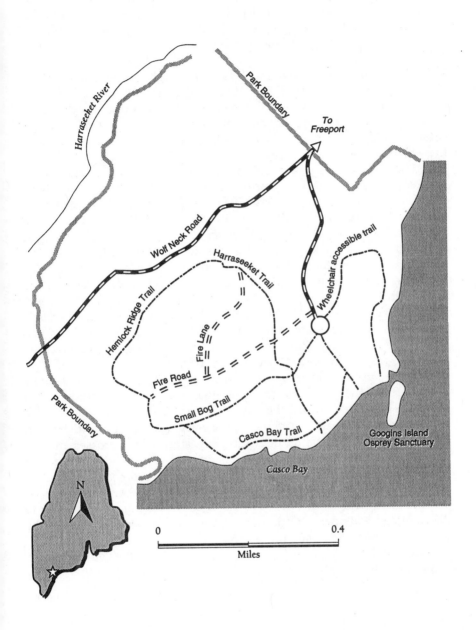

Finding the trailhead: From Bow Street in Freeport, take Flying Point Road to Wolf Neck Road, on the right. Go south 2.2 miles on Wolf Neck Road until you reach a large state park sign on the left. The trailhead is marked by a sign to the right of the parking lot. Alternative parking is available on the shoulder of the road near a field.

The hike: From the informational sign, head right on the **Harraseeket Trail**, slightly past the trailhead. The trail is narrow but well defined, winding through spruces and white birches. At 0.2 mile, go straight across a four-way intersection. Shortly down the trail you come to a log footbridge. After the bridge, the trail becomes rough. Footing can be tricky because of the web of spruce roots intertwined over the trail.

At 0.4 mile, cross a power line and go straight. The trails are not blazed, so refer to the map in this book or the one in the state park pamphlet. Soon you will come to a hemlock forest. Cross a corduroy road and a sign for the Harraseeket Trail. Go left here on the **Hemlock Ridge Trail** into a peaceful hemlock woods. In the winter, snow is not as deep under the trees as in other areas, making life easier for deer and other mammals. An interpretive sign on the trail here tells of rocks, hemlocks, and the Ice Age.

At 0.7 mile is the intersection of the Harraseeket Trail on the right and the **Small Bog Trail** and **Casco Bay Trail** on the left. Go left to the Casco Bay Trail. The trail leaves the hemlocks and heads downhill. Cross a classic stone fence and head into mixed white birches and firs. Partridge berry and bunchberry plants cover the ground here. At 0.8 mile, cross an old fire road. You can see down to Casco Bay on the right.

The trail passes some large oaks. At 0.9 mile the Small Bog Trail enters on the left and the Casco Bay Trail continues dead ahead. Go straight. The trail goes downhill toward the bay. Cross another bridge and follow a cobblestone walk to a promontory, where you can look out over the water.

From here, continue on the Casco Bay Trail, which crosses another wooden bridge. At 1.3 miles, the trail is directly atop a bluff. Go through a narrow path lined with white and red pines and come to another outlook and informational sign. Gray squirrels are numerous here because oaks provide them with acorns, their favorite food. At 1.5 miles, take a spur to the right and walk down to the water. Another sign stands near a rocky ledge, describing the life on the shore.

Back on the trail, you are nearing the parking lot as the path is covered with gravel. At 1.6 miles you are back at the trailhead.

HIKE 46   *MAST LANDING*

General description: A hike through an Audubon sanctuary with upland ridges, fields, and a tidal stream.
General location: On the outskirts of Freeport in Cumberland County.
Maps: The Maine Audubon Society trail map of Mast Landing is available at the sanctuary; see also DeLorme's *The Maine Atlas and Gazetteer*, Map 6.
Degree of difficulty: Easy.
Length: 1.9 miles on various trails.
Elevations: No significant elevations encountered.
Water availability: Bring your own water.
Special attractions: Mast Landing gives visitors a glimpse of what Maine looked like in the past. The word "mast" refers to an industry that once flourished here: mast-making for sailing ships. The many mature oaks produce another kind of mast today: acorns.

The trails at Mast Landing provide opportunities to view upland game and birds as well as estuarine wildlife. The trail guide available at the trailhead offers insights on the area's natural history. This hike is highly recommended for families with children.
Best season: Year-round.
For more information: Maine Audubon Society, 118 U.S. Highway 1, Gilsland Farm, Falmouth, ME 04015; (207) 781-2330.
Finding the trailhead: Take U.S. Highway 1 north through Freeport. Across from an L. L. Bean retail outlet in the center of town look for Bow Street. Turn right. Follow Bow Street to the bottom of a hill, where the road crosses a small stream. Just past the stream, look for the Upper Mast Landing Road on the left. A sign directs you to the Audubon sanctuary. The trailhead is at the left of the parking lot near a directory.

The hike: The hike begins on **Orchard Trail**, which goes right as you enter the woods at the trailhead. Please log in at the registration box here. The trail is marked with blue blazes and goes through reverting farmland, with small pines growing along the edges of old fields. Ground juniper has taken hold here, too.

At 0.2 mile you come to an intersection and a stone fence on the left. Bear right for the **Deer Run Trail**, near a stand of red sumac. The trail goes along the bottom of a hillside. The woods here are mixed white pines and oaks. The trail narrows and, at 0.5 mile, enters a monoculture of white pines with no underbrush or understory trees.

At 0.6 mile, you come to another fork. Bear right on the **Link Trail**. The trail goes over a bank, where you can look down on a gully. At 0.8 mile, take the **Ridge Trail**. Go right here and at 0.9 mile, you will pass the beginning of the **Bench Loop**, a short diversion that begins and ends at this spot. If you do not take the Bench Loop, continue on and bear left to a field,

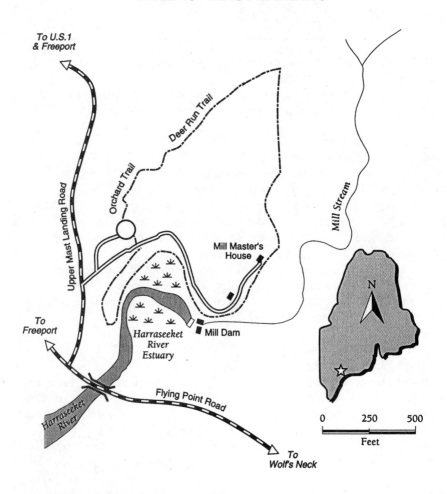

where you go right for the **Mill Stream Trail**. Signs of deer are plentiful in this long, narrow field.

Pass the Mast Landing Nature Camp building and the program building, at 1 mile, then pass the mill master's house and walk down a gravel road. To the left is the site of a fallen-down gristmill. You can walk out on the granite retaining wall to the breach. A picnic table at the mill site is an inviting spot to have lunch.

At 1.4 miles, a sign on the left indicates the **Estuary Trail**. Go left over several small wooden bridges that span small rivulets and along the edge of the estuary. Look for deer beds, areas where grass is matted down. Be warned that even in September the mosquitoes are active near the estuary. At 1.5 miles, a bench overlooking the estuary provides a place to sit.

The trail crosses another wooden bridge and becomes steep, necessitating the use of wooden ladders placed on the ground. At the top of a bluff, the trail reaches **Hawthorn Spur** on the left. This spur gives you a better overview of the estuary, if you choose to walk it. Continue on and go to the right on the Estuary Trail, which doubles back on itself. Here you can look down upon the estuary and the path you just took. At 1.9 miles, the Estuary Trail brings you back to the parking lot.

HIKE 47   RACHEL CARSON NATIONAL WILDLIFE REFUGE, UPPER WELLS DIVISION

General description: A self-guided interpretive trail around a salt marsh.
General location: Between Wells and Kennebunkport in York County.
Maps: A trail guide is available at the refuge; see also DeLorme's *The Maine Atlas and Gazetteer*, Maps 2 and 3.
Degree of difficulty: Easy.
Length: 1-mile loop.
Elevations: No significant elevations encountered.
Water availability: Bring your own water.
Special attractions: Salt marshes are uncommon in Maine because most of the coastline is unprotected from heavy waves; the grasses that build marshes need a stable environment. So these marshes, protected by the Rachel Carson National Wildlife Refuge, are environmental treasures. The

Barrier-free observation platform.

HIKE 47 RACHEL CARSON NATIONAL WILDLIFE REFUGE, UPPER WELLS DIVISION

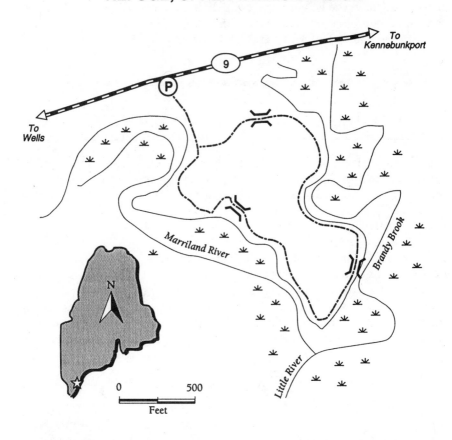

educational value and sheer beauty of this hike makes it a must for families with children, and the walk is accessible to people in wheelchairs.

Best season: Year-round.

For more information: Refuge leaflets can be obtained at refuge headquarters, open 8 a.m. to 4:30 p.m. each day in summer, closed weekends in winter. Or contact the Refuge Manager, Rachel Carson NWR, Rural Route 2, Box 751, Wells, ME 04090; (207) 646-9226.

Finding the trailhead: From Wells, take U.S. Highway 1 northeast to its intersection with Maine Route 9. Turn right onto ME 9. Within 1 mile from the intersection, look for a large wooden sign indicating the Rachel Carson National Wildlife Refuge on the right. Turn by this sign and park in a small lot. To the right of the lot is a trail sign; this is the trailhead.

The hike: Walk past the trail sign on a barrier-free gravel path. On the immediate right is a salt marsh, and on the left are piney woods. Walk to the edge of the marsh where the trail goes right and left. Go left to an observation post under a large hemlock tree near a wooden footbridge.

Continue on the trail and you will come to another observation point at the edge of the marsh on a stream bank; Branch Brook flows directly underneath. From here the trail bears right and makes a small loop around a marsh inlet.

At 0.5 mile, you come to another observation point, where you can look out across the greater part of the salt marsh, toward the sea. The trail leads downhill from here. There are handholds for people in wheelchairs. At the bottom of the hill, an observation platform is built directly over the water, so that at high tide Branch Brook flows directly beneath your feet.

From the platform the trail bears right and doubles back toward the parking lot. You will reach a point where you can see open ocean. A boulder with a brass plaque here is dedicated to Rachel Carson and her lifework. Soon you will pass another lookout. Next the trail crosses a gully by means of a wooden footbridge. You will pass one last observation point, from which you can see straight out into the sea as well as into the marsh by the Merriland River. The trail then goes back to the beginning of the loop and ends at the parking lot.

In the same day, you may want to take a nearby hike just a few miles up ME 9. The **Bridle Path**, a trail on an abandoned railroad bed, crosses the highway here. You can park on the left across from a small building surrounded by chainlink fence. On the right side of the road, you can walk down a narrow path on the edge of the refuge. The path crosses a tidal stream, which presents no problem at low tide. This is a popular local hike.

HIKE 48 *WELLS RESERVE AT LAUDHOLM FARM*

General description: The Wells Reserve is an old Maine saltwater farm. The hikes here cover fields, forests, salt marches, and beaches.
General location: Between Wells and Kennebunkport in York County.
Degree of difficulty: Easy.
Length: Saltmarsh Loop is 1.4-miles, plus 7 miles of other loop and interpretive trails.
Elevations: No significant elevations encountered.
Water availability: Water is available in rest rooms April-October. Bring your own water other times.
Special attractions: A visitor center offers brochures, trail maps, various exhibits, a slide show, and guided tours of the trail system. Guided tours are offered daily and require reservations. A calendar of special events such as wetland tours, bird walks and bandings, and wildflower tours is available. This hike, like the Rachel Carson National Wildlife Refuge trail, is highly recommended for families with children. A portion of the Laird-Norton Trail is barrier-free.
Best season: Year-round. The reserve is open daily, 8 a.m. to 5 p.m. The visitor center is open from 10 a.m. to 4 p.m. Monday through Saturday,

Laird Norton Interpretive Trail, Laudholm Farm.

and from 12 p.m. to 4 p.m. Sunday, May through October. It is open from 10 a.m. to 4 p.m. Monday through Friday for the balance of the year.
For more information: Wells National Estuarine Research Reserve, Rural Route 2, Box 806, Wells, ME 04090; (207) 646-1555.
Finding the trailhead: From Wells, take the Maine Turnpike to Exit 2 and turn left. Continue to a set of traffic lights and turn left onto U.S. Highway 1. Proceed for 1.5 miles, then take a right on Laudholm Farm Road by the second blinking light. Take the first left to the reserve entrance.

The hike: Beginning at the visitor center, follow the driveway to the flag-pole and turn left at a sign indicating the **Knight Trail**. The trail begins in a hayfield with a cedar post fence on the right. In September, the field is full of toadflax (also called butter-and-eggs), wild snapdragons, and New England asters and fall dandelions.

Turn right at the end of the field and walk down a hill while watching for deer at the bottom. On the left and right of the trail are apple trees and shrubs. The trail goes down hill, through sweet ferns and bayberry bushes. At the bottom of the hill turn left onto a wooden boardwalk.

At a wooden bridge, the **Pilger Trail** begins on the right, and the **Laird-Norton Trail** is on the left. Take the Laird-Norton Trail 0.9 mile to a beach outlook with views of the salt marsh, river mouth, double barrier beach, as well as ocean surf. The boardwalk is posted with informational signs telling the natural history of these woods.

HIKE 48   WELLS RESERVE AT LAUDHOLM FARM

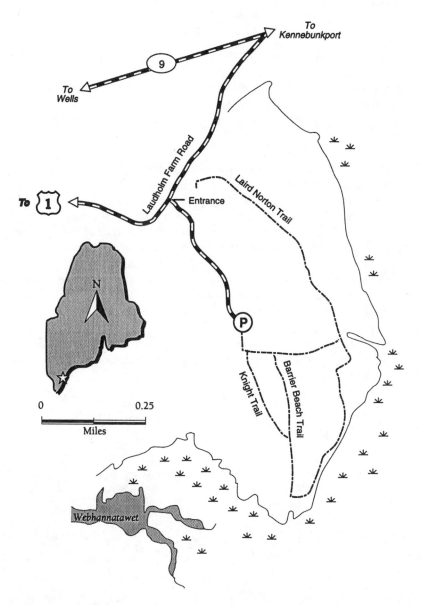

Still on the boardwalk, you walk through mixed red maple and gray birches. Finally, you come out in the open and turn left toward the visitor center at 1.1 miles. You will walk up an old farm lane with the visitor center in view. At 1.4 miles you arrive back at the trailhead.

The Wells Reserve at Laudholm Farm has 7 miles of interpretive trails, so you can easily spend an entire day exploring the woods, fields, dunes, ocean, and salt marsh. If you come in summer, be sure to carry insect repellent.

HIKE 49 *MARGINAL WAY*

General location: A village hike along a mile-long headland on the Atlantic Ocean.
General location: The town of Ogunquit, about 12 miles north of the New Hampshire border, in York County.
Maps: DeLorme's *The Maine Atlas and Gazetteer*, Maps 1 and 2.
Degree of difficulty: Easy.
Length: 1 mile round-trip.
Elevations: No significant elevations encountered.
Water availability: Bring your own water.
Special attractions: Marginal Way is probably the most popular village walk in Maine. The village of Ogunquit is a famous tourist town, full of curio shops and fine restaurants. The walk along Marginal Way is a fitting end to a day of shopping and eating. The ocean views here are unparalleled, and if you come here on a stormy day with an onshore wind, you can see the wrath of the open ocean as it batters the rocky shore. This setting would appeal to a filmmaker shooting a scary mystery. In fact, Marginal Way is a favored spot for artists, naturalists, and photographers.
Best season: Year-round.
For more information: Consult DeLorme's *The Maine Atlas and Gazetteer*, or pick up a copy of *The Tourist News*, a free publication available at most stores in Ogunquit.

Along Marginal Way, Ogunquit.

HIKE 49 MARGINAL WAY

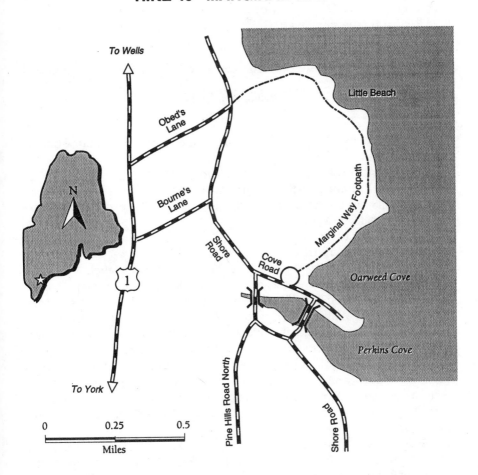

Finding the trailhead: Take U.S. Highway 1 to Ogunquit. Perkins Cove is the trailhead, but parking may be limited in summer. You might want to park in town and walk south on Shore Road to Cove Road. Look for a sign indicating the Marginal Way footpath across from Barnacle Billy's Restaurant.

The hike: The path winds around the head of Oarweed Cove and bears right on a rocky headland. As you walk, the rocky shoreline is directly below you, and a side hill covered with pasture roses is on your left.

You walk atop rocky cliffs, but there are plenty of opportunities to climb down to the water's edge. Be careful doing this in stormy weather, since the current is strong and a swimmer would have little chance of making it back to shore.

Near the end of the trail, you come to a promontory, a favorite place to sit and take in the ocean scenery. A beacon marks the official end of the trail. Whenever you come, bring a camera, since you will definitely want to preserve memories of the stirring scenery.

Return by the same path.

HIKE 50   *KENNEBUNKPORT*

General description: A seaside walk in one of southern Maine's most noted villages.

General location: Kennebunkport in York County.

Maps: The Kennebunk-Kennebunkport Chamber of Commerce can provide a map of the Kennebunk villages; see also DeLorme's *The Maine Atlas and Gazetteer*, Map 3.

Degree of difficulty: Easy.

Length: 1 mile round-trip.

Elevations: No significant elevations. The hike is at sea level.

Water availability: No water, except at shops and restaurants.

Special attractions: The hike takes you past former President and Mrs. George Herbert Walker Bush's home at Walker Point. Views include a panoramic look at the Kennebunk River, the Atlantic Ocean, and on a clear day, Mount Agamenticus, a lone mountain to the south.

Best season: Year-round, but Spouting Rock and Blowing Cave are most impressive during an incoming tide or storm, when the sea is restless.

For more information: Kennebunk-Kennebunkport Chamber of Commerce, P.O. Box 740, Kennebunk, ME 04043-0740; (207) 967-0858, or (207) 967-0857.

Finding the trailhead: From points south, take U.S. Highway 1 north to Maine Route 9 and head east on ME 9 for Kennebunkport. Once there, follow ME 9 to Ocean Avenue. Look for a sign on the right directing you to parking for the beach. Drive down this road and park. This is the trailhead.

The hike: You can walk along the beach first to stretch your legs for the hike. For the trail, walk out of the parking lot and turn right along Ocean Avenue with its Victorian houses. The first place of interest is Parson's Park on the right. This small oceanside park offers good views of the ocean, the Kennebunk River, and sometimes Mount Agamenticus to the south.

Proceed along the trail and around a bend, where you will confront the open ocean. Here, with an onshore wind, you can experience the power and fury of the Atlantic in all its glory. If you are here at half tide, you can observe a natural fountain known as Spouting Rock. A large crevice has been carved out by the elements; as the tide forces rolling waves into the crevice, a tall plume of spray is ejected far into the air.

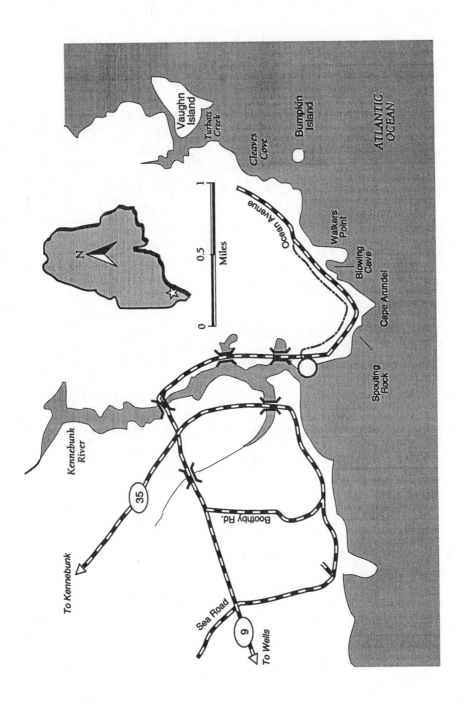

At the Kennebunkport trailhead.

Continue on the trail to observe Blowing Cave. Similar in nature to Spouting Rock, this ocean cave is nearly 16 feet long and 8 feet deep. The roar of waves being forcefully ejected from the cave can be heard for a great distance.

Finally on the right you can see Walker's Point and the Bush home, with the American flag prominently displayed. After you pass Walker's Point, the hike winds away from the ocean. Follow your steps back to the trailhead.

General description: A hike on a woodland loop and to the summit of a lone mountain.

General location: Near Pownal Center inland from North Yarmouth in Cumberland County.

Maps: A map is available at the state park or from the Bureau of Parks and Recreation; see also DeLorme's *The Maine Atlas and Gazetteer*, Map 5.

Length: 1.3-mile loop plus 0.2 mile round-trip to the summit.

Elevations: 484 feet at the summit.

Water availability: Water is available at the park.

Special attractions: Bradbury Mountain State Park is a quiet, attractive park in southern Maine, not far from several other trailheads. Woodland campsites here offer relative seclusion. The trails are never crowded.

Best season: Year-round.

For more information: Bureau of Parks and Recreation, Maine Department of Conservation, State House Station 22, Augusta, ME 04333; (207) 289-3821.

Finding the trailhead: From Yarmouth, take Maine Route 9 north to Pownal Center. Just past the village center, look for a sign for the Bradbury Mountain State Park camping area on the right. Day-use parking is on the left, across from the camping area. Park here; this is the trailhead.

Old cattle pound at Bradbury Mountain State Park.

HIKE 51 BRADBURY MOUNTAIN STATE PARK

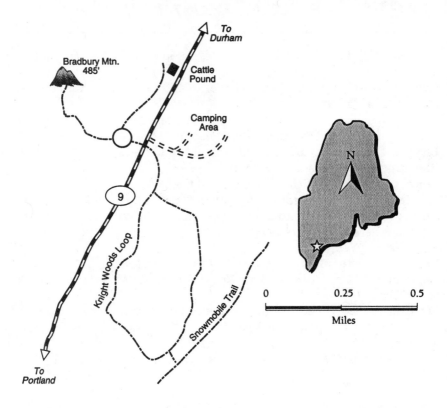

The hike: The **Knight Woods Loop**, a new trail, begins across from the parking lot. It is marked by a sign with a picture of a hiker.

The trail goes through a pine grove with a stone wall on the left. At the first fork in the trail, take a right. This trail is marked with white blazes nailed to the trees. The trail here is smooth and carpeted with pine needles.

At 0.1 mile, you can go left or right. Go left. This begins the loop. The rock wall here is of some antiquity, built when the town was first laid out and the land was first cleared, a testimony to the diligence of the early settlers. At 0.2 mile the trail bears right at the end of the stone fence. Now you are in a beech woods. The beeches show signs of blight, a disease that is slowly killing most eastern beeches. Only the youngest trees have escaped the infestation. Since this is a new trail, you can still see remnants of ashes where workers burned brush while clearing it.

At 0.4 mile, the trail goes into a stand of hemlocks. The trail is well marked. High winds have partially torn a large hemlock limb from the trunk where at press time it remained, hanging 15 feet in the air. Don't walk under this limb. On the left, you can see low ground, a swampy area.

At 0.5 mile, you come to a plank bridge. Cross the bridge and look around on the knoll. Notice the openness of the woods. There is very little understory here, enabling you to see a good distance. Leaving the hemlocks, the road goes downhill and into some small hardwoods. On the left, a red maple has a white marker, and past here, a huge boulder shows glacial scratching. The boulder is covered with staghorn lichen.

The trail goes steadily downhill now—this would be great terrain for cross-country skiing. As you continue walking, you can begin to hear traffic on the main road. At 0.6 mile, go right at a fork. Cross a wooden bridge over a small brook, and walk through peaceful piney woods. Just to the right of the trail is a wolf pine, a giant of a tree with so many limbs that it would be too knotty for good lumber. This is the largest tree in the area.

At 1.1 miles the trail goes through a hemlock grove. There are traces of red paint on trailside rocks, probably guides for the trail builders. At 1.2 miles, you are back to the beginning of the loop; at 1.3 miles, you reach the parking area.

Now for the mountain. Walk across the parking area, following the white blazes. At the edge of the parking area, a sign indicates the beginning of the **Summit Trail**. Ground juniper lines the trail, and you pass a double white ash tree. The trail becomes steep as you pass a granite ledge. The trail gets considerably steeper and could be slippery in wet weather. It bears left, going over more of the ledge. Workers have placed large, flat stones, to make steps here. On the right, you can see glacial scratches on a large boulder.

The trail bears left and opens to the rocky summit of Bradbury Mountain. Looking down and across, you can see the scope of the woods where you walked on the Knight Woods Loop. A quick glance shows you why it is important to stay on marked trails. Far to the right is a farmhouse with a large barn. Other views include Mount Washington, Casco Bay, and parts of Lake Sebago. This is the highest point for miles around. Retrace your route to the parking lot.

HIKE 52   *GILSLAND FARM*

General description: Trails through open fields, woodlands, and along the Presumpscot River estuary in a sanctuary maintained by the Maine Audubon Society.

General location: In Falmouth, just a few miles north of Portland in Cumberland County.

Maps: A trail map is available at the sanctuary; see also DeLorme's *The Maine Atlas and Gazetteer*, Map 5.

Degree of difficulty: Easy.

Length: 1.2-mile loop, with a total of 2.5 miles of trail in the sanctuary.

Elevations: No significant elevations.

Water availability: Water is available at the visitor center.

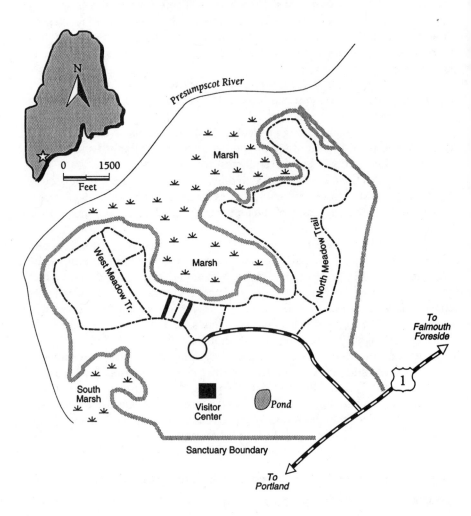

Special attractions: Gilsland Farm is a diverse natural community. The visitor center is the site of nature-related exhibits. The reading library and conference room contains a large collection of mounted specimens of Maine birds and mammals, including several extinct species. The teacher's resource center loans a wide variety of materials dealing with environmental topics, and the Maine Audubon store sells a variety of items dealing with the environment and Maine's natural history. The Goduti Wildlife Garden, near the visitor center, is designed to attract birds and small mammals. A brochure describes the garden and gives tips on landscaping for wildlife.

This hike is perfect for families with children. The walking is easy, and the educational materials available provide a wealth of natural history information.

For more information: Maine Audubon Society, Gilsland Farm, 118 U.S. Highway 1, Falmouth, ME 04105; (207) 781-2330.

Finding the trailhead: From Portland, drive north on U.S. Highway 1. Watch for the Gilsland Farm sanctuary sign on the left, opposite the intersection of U.S. 1 and Maine Route 88. Alternately, travel south on ME 88 from Falmouth as far as its intersection with U.S. 1 and watch for the sign on the immediate right.

The hike: Look for a trail sign just north of the visitor center. Walk past the sign and down a wood-chip-covered trail to a four-way intersection. Turn right at this intersection and follow the trail along a stone fence. Turn right to the **North Meadow Trail.**

At this point, you can see the Presumpscot River directly ahead. Continue on the trail through oak trees.

Now the trail goes up a slight hill and into an open meadow. A footbridge takes you over a wet spot. The trail bends toward the saltwater. Down by the water, you can see where rivulets have carved channels through the mudflats on their way to the river. Double-crested cormorants fly up and down the river here. With views of Portland's skyline in the distance, you are compelled to wonder what this place would be like were it not for the generosity of the previous owner and the gentle care of the Maine Audubon Society.

The trail follows the shoreline. You will soon have to step over an active woodchuck den. You then pass a thick hedgerow of pasture roses, laden with rosehips in September. Just past the roses, the trail dips to a point where you have the impression of being in a vast bowl.

The trail bears sharply to the right and is lined with red sumacs. The trail then leaves the shore and winds through North Meadow and toward the community gardens. From here, you can look back and see the meadow and the route you just traced.

HIKE 53   *HOCKOMOCK NATURE TRAIL*

General description: A self-guided nature trail through woods and fields and along the shore.

General location: Keene Neck south of Waldoboro in Bremen, Lincoln County.

Maps: Pick up a trail guide at the visitor center or by writing to the National Audubon Society Ecology Camp, Keene Neck Road, Medomak, ME 04551; see also DeLorme's *The Maine Atlas and Gazetteer*, Map 7.

Degree of difficulty: Easy.

Length: 1-mile loop.

Elevations: No appreciable elevations encountered.

The hulk of the *Cora Cressy*, center, as seen from the Hockomock Trail.

Water availability: Bring your own water.

Special attractions: The trail passes an example of an Indian shell midden. People of the Abnaki Tribe summered on Keene Neck, digging shellfish and depositing the shells in heaps. The Audubon Ecology Camp has dug into one of these heaps, exposing layers of clamshells that date from the years before European colonization.

Best season: Year-round.

For more information: National Audubon Society, Audubon Ecology Camp, Keene Neck Road, Medomak, ME 04551; Audubon Ecology Camps and Workshops, National Audubon Society, 613 Riversville Road, Greenwich, CT 06831.

Finding the trailhead: From U.S. Highway 1 in Waldoboro, take Maine Route 32 south to Bremen. Just after a cemetery on the right, look for an Audubon Society Ecology Camp sign on the right. Turn here, on Keene Neck Road; the road sign is set back and obscured by brush. Follow Keene Neck Road for 2 miles until you come to the Audubon camp. The trailhead is on the right, just past the visitor center. Be sure to pick up a trail guide.

The hike: Look for a sign at the right of a dirt road just past the visitor center. The sign indicates the trailhead for the **Hockomock Trail**. Walk through a meadow and soon you will come to a stone fence. This meadow was cleared by colonial settlers in the 1700s, who erected the stone fence with rocks pulled from the meadow to facilitate plowing.

HIKE 53   HOCKOMOCK NATURE TRAIL

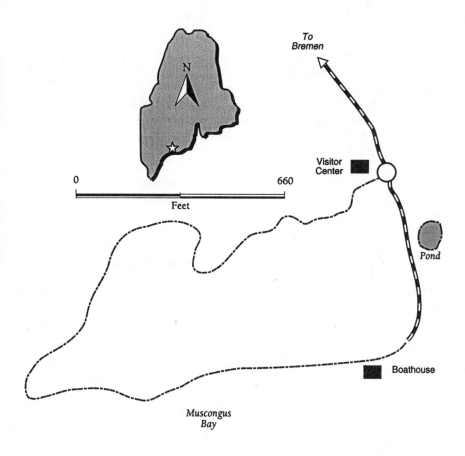

The trail goes through a stand of 50-year-old paper birches, then leaves the birch stand and goes by an ancient red oak. Crossing another stone fence, the trail goes through a forest of mature red spruces. Wildflowers and mosses abound in the filtered sunlight beneath the trees.

Leaving the spruce forest, the trail leads past a 150-year-old white pine and to the seashore. Here, on the left of the trail, is where a shell midden left by the Abnaki people has been opened to expose the layers of clamshells. Looking across the water, you can see the Audubon Ecology Camp on Hog Island. Look for sea ducks, double-crested cormorants, and herring gulls on the water.

The trail follows the wooded shoreline and re-enters the bottom of the meadow. Up ahead along the shore is the immense hull of the Cora Cressy, a five-masted schooner. This is the best preserved hull of such a ship in Maine. Follow the trail up the hill, through the meadow, past a small pond, and back to the visitor center.

ISLAND HIKES OVERVIEW

On our state's offshore islands, Mainers live a separate way of life. Connected to the mainland only by ferries, island people are obliged to plan ahead for their needs. If they miss the last ferry in the afternoon, they must wait until the next day to get across. That's a fact of life.

The astounding beauty of Maine's offshore islands, coupled with peace, tranquillity, and ever-present aromas and sounds of the sea, are ample reasons for modern islanders to be content to live here—often in the same house that their ancestors built several hundred years ago. Those same advantages attract large numbers of visitors each year.

Old ways and customs die hard in island societies. In years past, for instance, people meeting on the street always exchanged pleasantries or at least acknowledged each other in some way. In island Maine even today, you shouldn't be surprised when a stranger waves to you as you drive or hike along a road. Wave back. You might make a friend.

HIKE 54   *ISLESBORO*

General description: An island hike past stately homes, over a narrow ridge with ocean views on both sides, and around a rocky point with views of the open ocean.

General location: Opposite Lincolnville Beach in Waldo County, midcoast Maine.

Maps: DeLorme's *The Maine Atlas and Gazetteer*, Maps 14 and 15.

Degree of difficulty: Easy.

Length: 5.8 miles round-trip.

Elevations: No significant elevations encountered.

Water availability: No water, except at shops.

Special attractions: The short walk around the tip of Pendleton Point rivals any of the more famous coastal areas for majestic scenery. Warren Island State Park, near the west side of the island, offers rustic camping in a pristine environment. It can only be reached by boat.

Best season: Year-round.

For more information: Islesboro Town Office, Main Road, Islesboro, ME 04848; (207) 734-2253.

Finding the trailhead: Take the ferry from Lincolnville Beach to Islesboro Island. From the landing, take Ferry Road and turn right at the first intersection. Follow this road to its intersection with Main Road. Turn right on Main Road and proceed to Dark Harbor. Dark Harbor is the trailhead. Alternately, you can park near the ferry landing and walk the entire distance, 13.5 miles round-trip. If you take the alternate hike, be sure to be-

Rockbound coast at Islesboro.

gin early in the morning so you can catch the last ferry to the mainland. In summer, the ferry is usually crowded, so allow yourself plenty of time.

The hike: Islesboro is a unique island community at the head of Penobscot Bay. Most of the island has long been settled, as attested to by the age and style of many of the homes, and summer residents have built stately mansions. As you walk or drive down the quiet roads here, people will wave to you, a friendly island tradition that persists even in this age of anonymity.

From the little village of Dark Harbor, walk south on Main Road. Soon, you come to a rise, giving you a look at the bay to the east. The road zig-zags and is lined on both sides by large spruces.

The road goes past small Cape Cod-style homes, a few large mansions, and a strictly modern structure before turning to gravel. Follow the gravel road to the town picnic area and the shoreline. At the shore, take the path to the left and walk on granite ledges at the water's edge. Pasture roses grow here, often wetted by salt spray.

Now you come to a head. To the left of the head, you can see a sharp inlet with a protected harbor. Follow the path around the head, past bayberry bushes, and return to the parking area. Follow your steps back to the trailhead.

HIKE 54 ISLESBORO

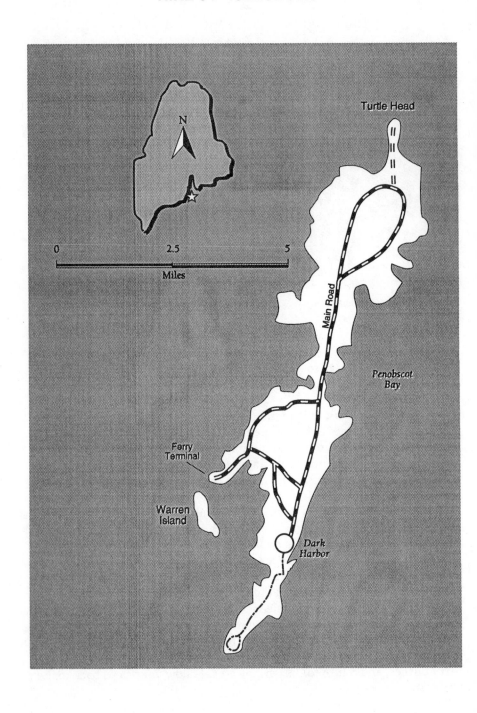

HIKE 55 *SEARS ISLAND*

General description: A hike around an uninhabited island connected to the mainland by a causeway.

General location: Northern Penobscot Bay near Searsport in Waldo County.

Maps: DeLorme's *The Maine Atlas and Gazetteer*, Map 14.

Degree of difficulty: Easy.

Length: 5-mile loop.

Elevations: Sea level, no significant elevations.

Water availability: Bring your own water.

Special attractions: The walk around Sears Island is actually a walking tour of the upper bay, since you get to look at area landmarks from every direction. Because of easy access, this is a popular hike with local residents. All the same, few bother to hike completely around the whole island.

Best season: Anytime. Although summer is the most popular time to do this hike, winter presents hikers with scenes of unmatched beauty.

For more information: Consult DeLorme's *The Maine Atlas and Gazetteer*.

Finding the trailhead: From Searsport, take U.S. Highway 1 north about 1.6 miles and look for a road to the right near a low, green building. Turn right and follow this road for 1.5 miles to a causeway. Park on either side

Secluded beach at Sears Island.

HIKE 55 SEARS ISLAND

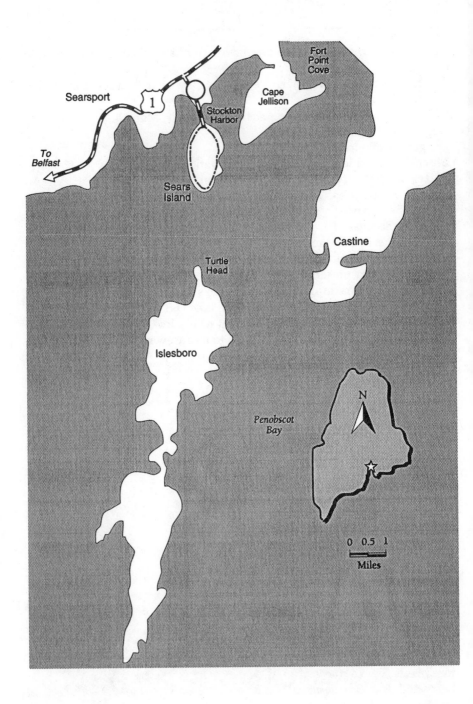

of the road at the far end of the causeway. This is the trailhead.

The hike: This wild island, owned by the State of Maine, is the continuing subject of controversy. A planned container port may or may not be built on the island's west side. Even if the port is built, the bulk of the island is slated to be left untouched—good news for all who love this remarkable place.

Leave the causeway on the left side and walk down to the shore. To your left is Kidder Point, and, past that, Stockton Harbor. After walking about 1 mile, you are opposite the southwestern tip of Cape Jellison. To the right of Cape Jellison is the mouth of the Penobscot River. Continuing along the shore brings you opposite Castine Peninsula, at about 2 miles.

As you round the southern tip of Sears Island, you can look to the south and get glimpses of open ocean to the left of Turtle Head on Islesboro Island. Coming around the west side of the island you can see Belfast and Searsport, and at 5 miles you are back at the causeway.

After completing the hike, you might like to drive a few miles up U.S. 1 and visit Cape Jellison and Fort Point State Park. The park contains a lighthouse, a fishing pier, the star-shaped foundation of old Fort Pownall, and many picnic tables along the water, and is rarely crowded.

HIKE 56   *GREAT WASS ISLAND*

General description: A day hike on the shore of a relatively undeveloped island managed by The Nature Conservancy (TNC).
General location: Just south of Jonesport in Washington County.
Maps: The Nature Conservancy provides a brochure mapping the island; see also DeLorme's *The Maine Atlas and Gazetteer*, Maps 17 and 26.
Degree of difficulty: Moderate. Trails can be dangerous in foul weather, especially during fog.
Length: 5-mile loop.
Elevations: Sea level; no significant elevations encountered.
Water availability: Bring your own water.
Special attractions: This 1,540-acre TNC island preserve is not been changed much by man. Some of its natural features are recognized by Maine's Critical Areas Program. The granite bedrock south shore shows evidence of the Fundian Fault, a crack in the earth's crust extending from New Hampshire to the Bay of Fundy.

Of all landmasses in eastern Maine, Great Wass Island extends the farthest out into the ocean. Here, the waters of the Bay of Fundy mix with those of the Gulf of Maine, producing a humid climate preferred by several rare plants. Two of these found in the island's raised bogs are baked-apple berry and dragon's mouth orchid.

HIKE 56 GREAT WASS ISLAND

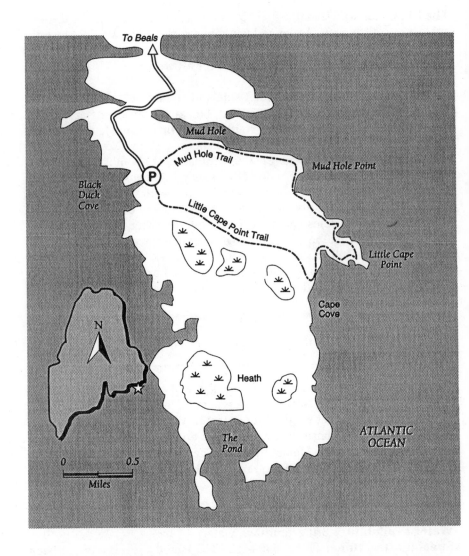

Wildlife is plentiful on the island. Ospreys and bald eagles hunt and roost on the island, and spruce grouse, upland birds usually found in the north woods, make their homes here.

Best season: Year-round, but April through November are the most pleasant.

For more information: Maine Chapter, The Nature Conservancy, Fort Andross, 14 Main Street, Suite 401, Brunswick, ME 04011; (207) 729-5181.

Finding the trailhead: From U.S. Highway 1, take Maine Route 187 to Jonesport. Go over the Beals Island Bridge at Moosabec Reach to the town of Beals, and from there head southeast to Great Wass Island. Follow the road, which turns to dirt, to Black Duck Cove about 3 miles from Beals. A marked parking area is on the left. Pick up a Great Wass Island preserve guide when you register.

The hike: The Nature Conservancy asks that visitors observe the following guidelines: Day use only. Please sign in at the registration box. No camping or fires, or pets. Stay on marked trails or on shoreline rocks. Public cooperation is needed to preserve the delicate natural balance of this special island environment.

The hike is a loop combining the **Mud Hole Trail**, the **Little Cape Point Trail**, and a section of shoreline. From the parking lot, the trail forks just a short distance in, with the Mud Hole Trail bearing left. Follow this trail through one of Maine's largest stands of jack pines. The trail then goes through a damp softwood forest just above the Mud Hole, a fjord-like cove. Continuing on, the trail bears south (right) and ends at Mud Hole Point, at 1.5 miles. The view from Mud Hole Point shows the islands of Eastern Bay.

To complete the loop, you must now walk along the shore toward Little Cape Point. Low tide is best for this part of the hike. It is 1.5 miles from the rock ledges of Mud Hole Point to Little Cape Point Trail. Walk along the shore, being careful to stay on rocks so as not to disturb what may be rare plant life.

Look for a cairn and red marker along the shore, indicating the beginning of the Little Cape Point Trail. This 2-mile trail goes over a "bog bridge," where you can study the carnivorous plants that grow here. Continuing past the bog, the trail winds through open ledges and softwood forests with a thick, mossy carpet, taking you back to your starting point.

HIKE 57 *BAR ISLAND*

General description: A day hike to an island reached by crossing a gravel bar at low tide.

General location: Bar Harbor on Mount Desert Island in Acadia National Park, Hancock County.

Maps: Maps of Acadia National Park and vicinity are available at the park from the National Park Service and from the USGS, Reston, VA 22092; see also DeLorme's *The Maine Atlas and Gazetteer*, Map 16.

Degree of difficulty: Easy.

Length: 1.5 miles round-trip.

Elevations: No significant elevations encountered.

Water availability: None, so bring your own.

Special attractions: The gravel bar for which Bar Harbor is named links Bar Island to the mainland. The island can be reached at low tide by foot and by motor vehicle, but driving across is **not** recommended.

Best season: Year-round.

For more information: Acadia National Park, Box 177, Bar Harbor, ME

HIKE 57 BAR ISLAND

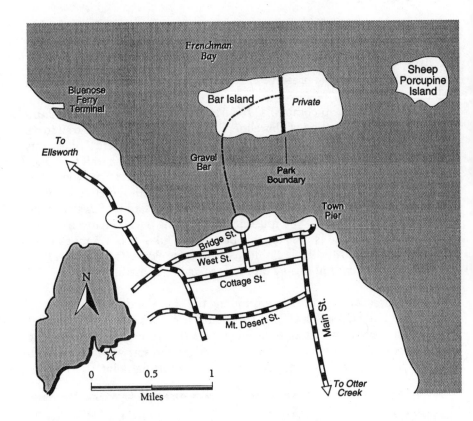

04609; (207) 288-3338, voice or TDD.
Finding the trailhead: From the Town Pier on West Street in Bar Harbor, walk 0.3 mile west to Bridge Street. The bar begins at the end of Bridge Street and goes about 0.5 mile to Bar Island.

The hike: Check the tide clock at the town pier before you set out for Bar Island. You will only have 2 to 3 hours to make the trip across and back. If you tarry on the island, you could be stranded for up to 8 hours. The possibility of getting stranded on an island adds a sense of adventure to the hike, but it can be an inconvenience, too.

From the end of Bridge Street, walk across the gravel bar. A camera and binoculars are good tools, since the bar is frequented by shorebirds and seabirds. The western half of Bar Island is park land, but the eastern half is privately owned, so upon reaching the island, bear left on an unmarked and unmaintained trail. Walk through a meadow to a high point on the island. From here you get a good view of Bar Harbor, Cadillac Mountain, and the other mountains in Acadia National Park. Return by the same route.

HIKE 58   *ISLE AU HAUT*

General description: A hike on forest and seaside trails on Isle au Haut in the Gulf of Maine.

General location: The Knox County section of Acadia National Park, 6 miles from Stonington on the mainland.

Maps: National Park Service map of Acadia National Park; DeLorme's *The Maine Atlas and Gazetteer*, Maps 9 and 15.

Degree of difficulty: Easy.

Length: 4.8 miles round-trip.

Elevations: No significant elevations encountered.

Water availability: Bring your own water.

Special attractions: The southern portion of Isle au Haut is part of Acadia National Park; the northern half of the island is privately owned. After completing the hike listed here, you might want to tour Isle au Haut's year-round fishing community.

Best season: May through October, but the boat to Duck Harbor runs only in the summer. Contact Acadia National Park authorities for assistance.

For more information: Acadia National Park, Bar Harbor, ME 04609; (207) 288-3338, voice or TDD.

Finding the trailhead: Isle au Haut can only be reached by boat. Taking the ferry from Stonington will allow you enough time for a day hike. If you wish to stay longer, make reservations for the use of a park lean-to by checking with the National Park Service. From the town landing on the island, turn right and drive to the ranger station. This is the trailhead.

The hike: Beginning at the ranger station, take the **Duck Harbor Trail**. At 1.4 miles, the trail reaches the shore at Moore Harbor on the west side of the island. After leaving Moore Harbor, the trail winds through a thick forest of spruces and firs, reaching the Duck Harbor Campground at 2.4 miles. From the campground, you can explore the shoreline at Duck Harbor. Return by the same route. Alternately, you can continue south from Duck Harbor on the **Loop Road** to the **Western Head Trail**, which takes you up on the cliffs at Western Head.

HIKE 58   ISLE AU HAUT

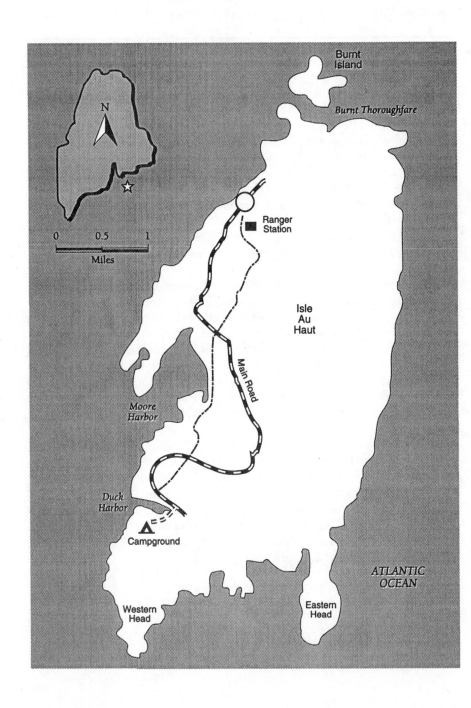

HIKE 59 *LITTLE CRANBERRY ISLAND*

General description: A hike along the beaches and roads of an offshore community.

General location: Islesford in the Cranberry Isles, about 2.5 miles south of the eastern section of Mount Desert Island, Acadia National Park.

Maps: Check the National Park Service map of Acadia National Park and the Appalachian Mountain Club map of Mount Desert Island; see also DeLorme's *The Maine Atlas and Gazetteer*, Map 16.

Degree of difficulty: Easy.

Length: 3 miles.

Elevations: No significant elevations encountered.

Water availability: Bring your own water.

Special attractions: The ferry docks at the village of Islesford which has

HIKE 59 LITTLE CRANBERRY ISLAND

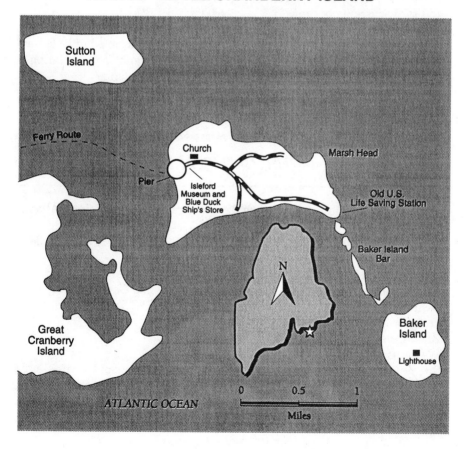

a seasonal restaurant on the dock, a general store, the Islesford Museum, and the Blue Duck Ship's Store, a historic store owned by Acadia National Park. The museum is open only in summer, when it is staffed by a park ranger. It contains photographs taken during the extreme winter of 1922-1923, when the ocean froze between the island and Northeast Harbor.

Best season: Year-round, as long as the ferry is running.
For more information: Call (207) 244-3575 for the current ferry schedule.
Finding the trailhead: Take the ferry to Little Cranberry Island from Northeast Harbor or Southwest Harbor on Mount Desert Island, Acadia National Park. The ferry landing at Islesford is the trailhead.

The hike: From the dock, follow the paved road out past the church and look for the second unpaved road to the left. Take this road to Back Beach on the south side of the island. This beach is a 0.5-mile expanse of pebbles, cobbles, and sand. The beach stretches east to the old U.S. Life Saving Service station. The station is now a private residence, so do not trespass. The U.S. Life Saving Service was the forerunner of the Coast Guard. It is probable that heroic rescues occurred here in years past.

At low tide, you will see the exposed bar leading to Baker Island. This bar is rocky and slippery, but with care you can walk out as far as the tide and swift currents permit.

Walk back to the church and look for the first dirt road to the left. Follow this road to its end, where you will see a recognizable but little-traveled trail to the right. This trail only goes a short distance before ending at a pebbled beach with a great view of Mount Desert Island.

Return to the trailhead by the same route. Alternately, you can follow the rocky, undeveloped shoreline for another 0.25 mile to Marsh Head.

HIKE 60   *MONHEGAN ISLAND*

General description: A hike along the headlands of one of Maine's Atlantic islands.
General location: Monhegan Island, about 11 miles south of Port Clyde in Knox County.
Maps: Maps of the trails are available on the island. Stop at the store and ask for assistance; see also DeLorme's *The Maine Atlas and Gazetteer*, Map 8.
Degree of difficulty: Cathedral Woods Trail, easy; Cliff Trail, fairly difficult.
Length: 1.5 miles.
Elevations: No significant elevations encountered.
Water availability: Bring your own water.
Special attractions: In spring, birders flock to Monhegan to witness the spring migration, when up to 100 different species can be seen in a day. The headlands on the island's north and east shores rise as high as 160 feet. Although camping is not allowed, three seasonal inns on Monhegan take

guests by reservation.

Best season: May through November.

For more information: A boat schedule from Port Clyde to Monhegan is available by contacting Monhegan Boat Line, P.O. Box 238, Port Clyde, ME 04855; (207) 372-8848. And for a summer schedule from Boothbay Harbor contact Balmy Days, Boothbay Harbor, ME 04538; (207) 633-2284.

Finding the trailhead: Take the ferry from Port Clyde or Boothbay Harbor to Monhegan. Once there, you will find several trails on the island, all of them numbered, with green markers nailed to trees at the trailheads. Look closely to see them. They begin from one or the other of two main roads on the island. The Cathedral Woods Trail, at marker 11, does not take much time, which is good if you have to worry about making the return trip on the ferry. From the ferry landing, go north past the schoolhouse and follow the main road. Near the end of the road, look for the trail marker on the right. This is the trailhead.

The hike: The Cathedral Woods Trail leaves the main road and enters a virgin forest, something uncommon in the east. As the trail bears northwest, spruce and fir trees create shade, even on a sunny day. Cathedral Woods is a unique natural area, with tall spruces, ferns, wildflowers, and lots of moss-covered boulders. It's truly a place to seek peace. The trail finally brings you to Squeaker Cove on the eastern shore, where you have an unobstructed view of the Atlantic Ocean.

If you have time, you also might want to do the **Cliff Trail**, which goes the length of the island. This is a fairly difficult trail, with some steep sections rising over numerous headlands. The Cliff Trail begins at the end of the main road on the left. Other trails intersect this trail as it winds around the island's southwest shore.

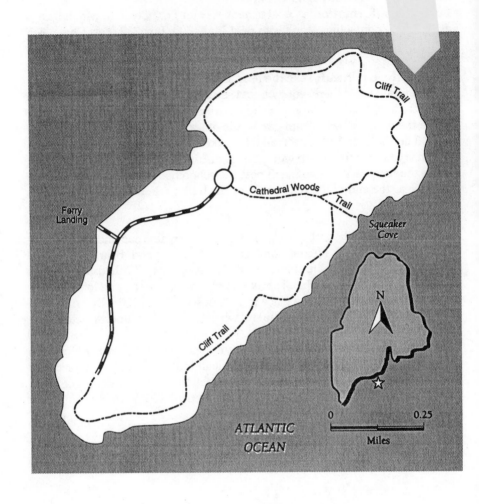

ACADIA AND MOUNT DESERT ISLAND HIKES OVERVIEW

The part of Maine called Acadia by the French and Americans, and New Scotland by the British, is the location of the only national park in Maine and the only true fjord in New England. Ocean air and water meet steep cliffs and high mountains in this fantastic land.

Mount Desert Island, the heart of Acadia National Park, offers seaside hikes as well as mountain trails leading to incomparable vistas. These trails and miles of carriage roads provide visitors with an almost unlimited choice of hikes in spring, summer, and fall. Private and public campgrounds, numerous motels, and cottages allow for extended stays in a variety of Acadia's magnificent settings. Hikers should call well in advance for reservations.

Entrance fees to Acadia National Park are $5 per vehicle, good for seven consecutive days, or $2 per person. An annual pass is available for $15.

Hikers in Acadia should be prepared for all types of weather. The ocean creates rain and fog here often, but temperatures may go as high as 85 degrees. Be sure to bring water-resistant clothing and insect repellent.

HIKE 61 *THE PRECIPICE*

General description: A short, rugged hike up a cliff to the summit of Champlain Mountain.

General location: Near the Sieur de Monts entrance to Acadia National Park, Mount Desert Island.

Maps: Maps of Acadia National Park are available at the park entrance (a brochure) or from the USGS. See also the Appalachian Mountain Club map of Mount Desert Island and DeLorme's *The Maine Atlas and Gazetteer*, Map 16.

Degree of difficulty: Difficult. Requires some bouldering and vertical ascents on iron rungs and ladders.

Length: 1.8 miles round-trip.

Elevations: The summit is 1,000 feet high.

Water availability: Bring your own water.

Special attractions: The Precipice is an exhilarating but challenging climb, even more difficult during wet weather or in ice and snow. Dogs are not allowed, and the hike is difficult for children.

Precipice Trail in Acadia National Park. *Photo by Will Harmon.*

HIKE 61 THE PRECIPICE

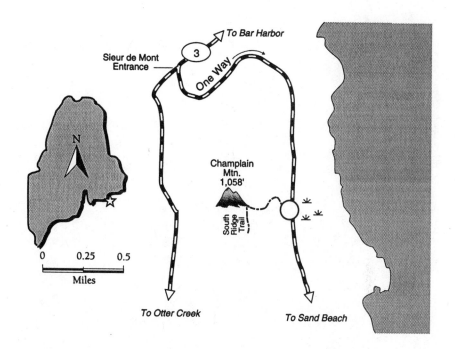

Best season: April through November.

For more information: Superintendent, Acadia National Park, P.O. Box 177, Bar Harbor, ME 04609; (207) 288-3338.

Finding the trailhead: From Bar Harbor on Mount Desert Island, drive south on Maine Route 3 for about 2 miles and turn right into the Sieur de Monts entrance to Acadia National Park. Pay the $5 entrance fee, which allows you access to the park for seven days. Follow signs indicating the Park Loop Road (a one-way road). Drive 2 miles on Park Loop Road until you come to the Precipice trailhead, on the left.

The hike: In summer, begin this hike before 10 a.m. to avoid crowds. This is a popular trail.

From the **Precipice** trailhead, look straight up from the base of the steps. The uppermost cliff face is negotiated by several sets of iron rungs and traverses narrow and sometimes sloping ledges. A few rungs and handrails are also scattered along the lower part of the trail, which runs 0.25 mile to the right then back to a point directly above the steps before climbing the ladders. As you climb, be careful not to dislodge loose rocks, for the safety of hikers below.

From the top of the steps, the trail continues up granite slabs and goes into a small patch of forest. Soon after this, you come to two iron rungs,

Precipice Trail in Acadia National Park. *Photo by Rose Harmon.*

used to climb an 8-foot-high wall. Beyond the wall, the trail continues in a northerly direction, crossing a boulder field with stone steps. You may have to scramble.

At the **East Face Trail** junction, make a hairpin turn to the south (left) and continue on a steeper trail. The first major set of iron rungs climbs the rock wall to your right at a spot where the trail briefly flattens. The next 0.2 mile is mostly vertical. The view of Frenchman Bay is excellent as long as it is not foggy.

As you climb, watch for endangered peregrine falcons. In the mid-1980s, hatchery chicks were released in the Jordan Cliffs area of Acadia. Between 1987 and 1990, peregrines returned to the Precipice. Park officials closed the trail for a month each year, hoping the birds would nest, but thus far no wild chicks have been hatched, so the trail has been reopened.

The cliff face ends, but the summit of Champlain Mountain still lies ahead. Follow cairns in a northerly direction across open ledges with scattered pines, watching for an obscure switchback to the left, near a 15-foot-high rock wall that runs north and south. Climb a few more rungs along this wall, and the summit cairn comes into view.

You can return by the same route. Alternately, you can take the **Bear Brook Trail** or the **South Ridge Trail** back to the Park Loop Road, coming out 1 mile from the Precipice trailhead.

HIKE 62 GREEN MOUNTAIN RAILROAD

General description: A hike along the route of the old cog railroad that once climbed Green (now Cadillac) Mountain.

General location: Just south of the Park Loop Road-Cadillac Mountain Summit Road junction, Acadia National Park, Mount Desert Island.

Maps: A map/brochure of Acadia National Park is available at the park entrance; see also the Appalachian Mountain Club map of Mount Desert Island and DeLorme's *The Maine Atlas and Gazetteer*, Map 16.

Degree of difficulty: Moderate. The railroad bed is not maintained, so it is steep and overgrown. The West Face Trail is steep, with many rock slabs that are slippery when wet.

Length: 2.5 miles.

Elevations: The summit of Cadillac is 1,530 feet above sea level.

Water availability: Bring your own water.

Special attractions: The Green Mountain Cog Railroad was only the second of its kind in the country. (The Mount Washington Cog Railroad in New Hampshire was the first.) Tourists first ascended the mountain by railroad in 1883. Business boomed thereafter: The railroad made four trips a day during the first year of operation. However, competition with the

HIKE 62 GREEN MOUNTAIN RAILROAD

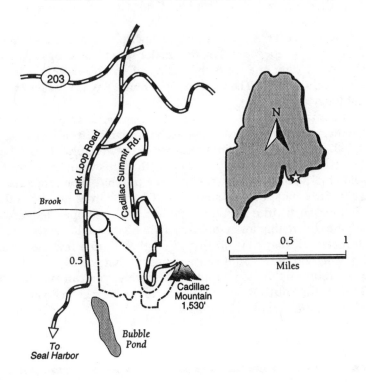

existing carriage road led to the railroad's decline. In 1895, the Green Mountain engines were sold to the Mount Washington Cog Railroad.

Best season: April through November.

For more information: Superintendent, Acadia National Park, P.O. Box 177, Bar Harbor, ME 04609; (207) 288-3338.

Locating the trailhead: Follow the Park Loop Road for 0.6 mile from its junction with the Cadillac Mountain Summit Road. Look for a paved pullout on the right. The pullout is the trailhead.

The hike: A brook crosses the road by the pullout. Follow this brook upstream for 100 yards and turn south, away from the brook. The old railroad bed is only a short distance from the brook. There is no maintained trail, but the route is obvious for most of the way. It is quite straight and easy to follow, though steep.

Vegetation can be a problem, especially after a rain or on a foggy day, when moisture clings to the leaves and branches. The trees that were cut down to make the route were used as fuel for the steam locomotives. The forest has not yet fully recovered.

You will discover more obvious signs of the railroad. Iron pins are still firmly embedded in the granite ledges. Do not pull out any pins or take any

At the summit of Cadillac Mountain.

loose metal found here, since historic artifacts are protected in Acadia National Park.

A 40-minute climb brings you to the Cadillac Mountain Summit Road. Follow this road to the top of the mountain and pick up the **South Ridge Trail** by the Park Gift Shop. Follow this trail to the junction with the **West Face Trail**. Turn right on the West Face Trail, which is very steep. The rock slabs may be slippery when wet. Descend on the trail to Bubble Pond and walk north on the Park Loop Road to the trailhead.

HIKE 63 *DORR MOUNTAIN*

General description: A hike through varied terrain around and up Dorr Mountain.

General location: The northeast corner of Mount Desert Island, Acadia National Park.

Maps: Maps of Acadia are available at the park entrance or from the USGS;

HIKE 63 DORR MOUNTAIN

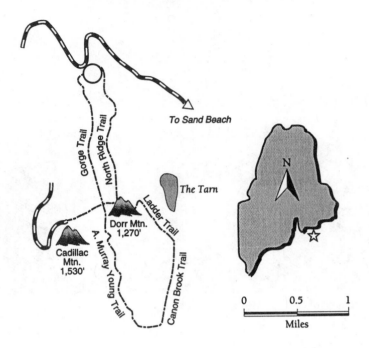

see also the Appalachian Mountain Club map of Mount Desert Island and DeLorme's *The Maine Atlas and Gazetteer*, Map 16.
Degree of difficulty: Relatively easy, but the trails are rough and rocky.
Length: 7.8 miles.
Elevations: Dorr Mountain rises 1,270 feet above sea level.
Water availability: Bring your own water.
Special attractions: Several trails on this loop contain outstanding examples of stonework, an enduring tribute to the early trail builders of Mount Desert Island.
Best season: April through November.
For more information: Superintendent, Acadia National Park, P.O. Box 177, Bar Harbor, ME 04609; (207) 288-3338.
Finding the trailhead: Enter Acadia National Park at the Sieur de Monts entrance. The trailhead for the Gorge Trail is about 1 mile from the beginning of the one-way section of the Park Loop Road. Look for a small gravel parking area on the right, just past Kebo Brook. The parking area is the trailhead.

The hike: The **Gorge Trail** begins at a highway bridge over Kebo Brook and crosses the brook twice as it wanders through hardwood forest. Eventually the trail returns to the brook and follows it up the valley. The Gorge for which the trail is named is small, but its cliffs attain heights of

172

40 feet. Because of the northerly exposure, ice remains here until early May.

At the saddle between Dorr and Cadillac Mountains, the hike continues straight ahead on the **A. Murray Young Trail**. The trail descends through an open meadow and follows a tributary of Canon Brook. Since watersheds on the island are small and underlain by granite ledges, the brooks and streams have little water in summer. If you do this hike after a heavy rain, you will better appreciate the waterfalls.

Not far from a plaque commemorating A. Murray Young is a trail junction. Continue straight toward Maine Route 3 and the Tarn, a small lake, passing another trail ascending the north ridge of Dorr Mountain. The trail turns north at some beaver ponds and follows the west side of the ponds north to the Tarn. You are actually on a great divide, since some of these ponds drain south to Otter Creek and others drain north.

Near the south end of the Tarn, turn left on the **Ladder Trail**, ascending Dorr Mountain. This trail is very steep, with hundreds of rock steps and only two small metal ladders to climb. The Ladder Trail joins the **Dorr Mountain Trail** from Sieur de Monts and continues up rock slabs, offering views of Frenchman Bay.

From the junction near the summit of Dorr Mountain, descend the **North Ridge Trail** to a saddle, then go up and over Kebo Mountain and continue going down to the Park Loop Road. When you reach the Park Loop Road, bear left and walk back to the trailhead, a distance of about 0.5 mile.

HIKE 64 *MANSELL MOUNTAIN*

General description: A day hike up Mansell Mountain, returning along the shore of Long Pond.

General location: Long Pond south of Somesville on Mount Desert Island, Acadia National Park.

Maps: Maps of Acadia are available at the park entrance and from the USGS; see also the Appalachian Mountain Club map of Mount Desert Island and DeLorme's *The Maine Atlas and Gazetteer*, Map 16.

Degree of difficulty: Moderate. The Perpendicular Trail has steep sections and rugged hiking to Great Notch.

Length: 5-mile loop.

Elevations: Mansell Mountain rises 949 feet above sea level.

Water availability: Bring your own water.

Special attractions: As with other hikes in Acadia National Park, this trail displays some fine examples of stonework.

Best season: April through November.

HIKE 64   MANSELL MOUNTAIN

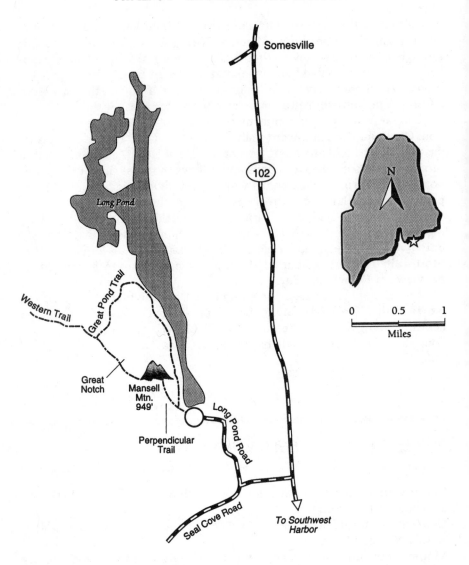

For more information: Superintendent, Acadia National Park, Box 177, Bar Harbor, ME 04609; (207) 288-3338, voice or TDD.

Finding the trailhead: From Somesville, take Maine Route 102 south to Seal Cove Road. Turn left on Seal Cove Road and continue until you reach its intersection with Long Pond Road. Turn left on Long Pond Road and follow it until it dead-ends at Long Pond. The Great Pond Trail begins at the south end of Long Pond behind the pumping station on the west side of the lake.

The hike: From the pumping station, follow the **Great Pond Trail** around the corner of the lake for only a short distance. Watch for the **Perpendicular Trail** branching off to the left, and follow it. The trail starts climbing immediately and soon crosses a boulder field, ascending the upper part with some remarkable switchbacks constructed entirely of stone. You will see many more beautifully constructed rock steps on this lower section of trail.

Getting closer to the summit of Mansell Mountain, you walk through a thick forest of spruces and firs. Here you begin to get a view to the east. From the summit, follow the signs for Bernard Mountain at the next two junctions.

From Great Notch, the hike descends northwesterly on the **Western Trail**, going through mature forest composed primarily of red spruces. You can see small spruces sprouting all over the forest floor. Now turn right on the Great Pond Trail, where you will encounter a gentle descent to Long Pond. At Long Pond, the trail turns south, following the shore back to the trailhead at the pumping station. If you want to take a swim, do it where you first approach the pond, since this is a public water supply and swimming is not permitted in the southern half.

HIKE 65   *GREAT HEAD*

General description: A hike on a sand beach and along oceanside cliffs.
General location: Great Head on the southeast coast of Mount Desert Island, Acadia National Park.
Maps: Maps of Acadia are available at the park entrance or from the USGS; see also DeLorme's *The Maine Atlas and Gazetteer*, Map 16.
Degree of difficulty: Generally easy, with some steep sections.
Length: 2 miles round-trip.
Elevations: No significant elevations encountered.
Water availability: Bring your own drinking water.
Special attractions: Sand beach is a rarity in this part of Maine. This is one of the few sandy, protected beaches in the area. The views of the mountains of Acadia and of offshore islands are breathtaking.
Best season: May through October.
For more information: Superintendent, Acadia National Park, Box 177, Bar Harbor, ME 04609; (207) 288-3338, voice or TDD.
Finding the trailhead: On Mount Desert Island, take Maine Route 3 south from Bar Harbor. Enter Acadia National Park at the Sieur de Monts entrance and look for the Park Loop Road. Continue south on the Park Loop Road to the Sand Beach parking area.

The hike: Walk down to the beach and head east, crossing a small stream flowing from a freshwater lagoon behind the beach. Head for the far corner

HIKE 65   GREAT HEAD

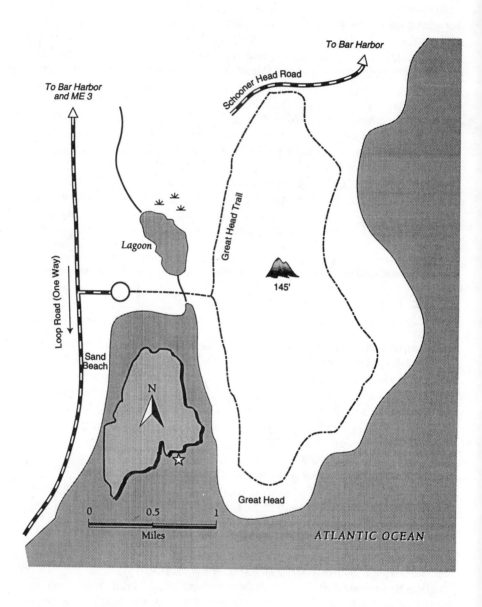

of the beach and look for a wooden trail post and stone steps leading up to a clearing with a huge millstone.

From here, the trail follows a wood road. At 0.2 mile from the millstone, turn right on a path marked by three white rocks. The trail curves, giving you a view of the sea. A side trail leads down to the ocean. Shortly after this, another side trail leads back to Sand Beach. Pass this and a group of white birches. Past the birches, the ground gets a bit swampy, but soon the trail winds over a ledge and brings you to the summit of Great Head. From here, you can see far out to sea. To the northeast are Schoodic Mountain and the Porcupine Islands in Frenchman Bay; to the southwest are Otter Cliffs, a few miles down the coast. At the summit is a bunch of rubble, all that remains of a stone teahouse.

From the ruins, the trail descends along the cliffs. The path is marked by stone cairns. The trail then climbs again, up the west side of Great Head. As you climb, you begin to get views of Sand Beach, the open sea, and the Beehive, a rock formation behind Sand Beach. Now the trail bears left by a stand of small pines and takes you back to the millstone, where you can retrace your steps to the trailhead.

HIKE 66 *SCHOODIC HEAD*

General description: A hike from a rocky, windswept shoreline to a mountaintop on the end of Schoodic Peninsula.
General location: In the section of Acadia National Park on the tip of Schoodic Peninsula on the mainland south of Winter Harbor in Hancock County.
Maps: Maps of Acadia are available at the park entrance and from the USGS; see also DeLorme's *The Maine Atlas and Gazetteer*, Map 17.
Length: 3.4 miles round-trip.
Elevations: The Schoodic Head summit is 440 feet above sea level.
Water availability: Bring your own water.
Special attractions: The views of Frenchman Bay and the rugged shoreline of Schoodic Point are well worth the short but steep hike to the summit. Schoodic Point is renowned for its stark shores and amazing surf. A day when the wind blows onshore is best to view this and an incoming tide.
Best season: May through November.
For more information: Superintendent, Acadia National Park, P.O. Box 177, Bar Harbor, ME 04609; (207) 288-3338, voice or TDD.
Finding the trailhead: From U.S. Highway 1 in West Gouldsboro, take Maine Route 186 south past Winter Harbor and follow signs for Acadia National Park, just past the village. Turn right at the park entrance and follow the signs for Schoodic Point. Watch for Blueberry Hill parking area on the right. The trailhead begins just before the parking area on the north side of the road.

Schoodic Point.

The hike: Look for a trailhead sign across the road from the parking area. The trail goes through an overgrown field, with alders, old apple trees, and red sumacs. At about 0.6 mile, the trail goes through several wet areas. Now the trail climbs a bit, passes a small pond, and comes to a gravel road at 0.8 mile. A warden's cabin is off to the right. Walk straight ahead on the gravel road and look for the **Schoodic Head Trail**, descending steeply toward you, on the right.

The trail heads east, climbing over boulders. After some even steeper climbing, the trail takes you to ledges and then a level area. After the level ground, the trail again rises steeply through a notch in the ledge and over a little brook.

At the top, after hiking for 1.7 miles, you are in a world of stunted jack pines and granite boulders. Here is one of the best views that Acadia can offer. Frenchman Bay sparkles below you, and the mountains on Mount Desert Island stand out clear and crisp. You can walk among the boulders and scrub at the top, but be sure to stay on the trail. Return to the trailhead by the same route.

HIKE 66 SCHOODIC HEAD

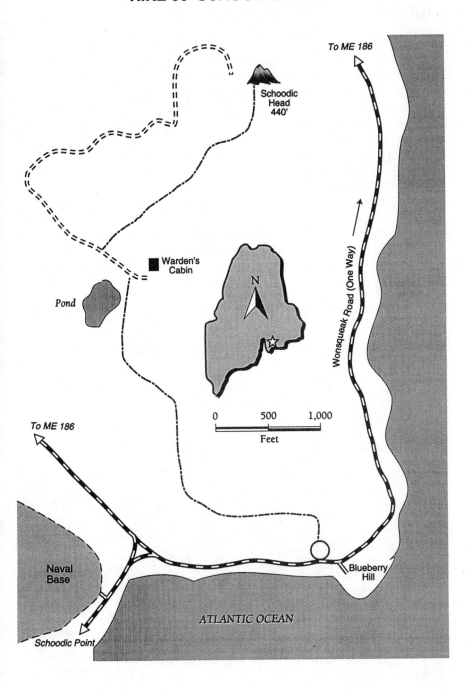

General description: A hike to a mountain summit featuring superb views of Mount Desert Island and the Atlantic Ocean.

General location: The eastern section of Mount Desert Island, Acadia National Park.

Maps: Maps of Acadia are available at the park entrance or from the USGS; see also the Appalachian Mountain Club map of Mount Desert Island and DeLorme's *The Maine Atlas and Gazetteer*, Map 16.

Degree of difficulty: Moderate.

Length: 2 miles round-trip.

Elevations: The Pemetic Mountain summit is 1,248 feet above sea level.

Water availability: Bring your own water.

Special attractions: Pemetic offers some of the best views of Mount Desert Island. The Pemetic Trail does not get as much pressure as some of the other hikes in the park, making it a perfect trail for the hiker seeking relative solitude.

Best season: April through November.

For more information: Superintendent, Acadia National Park, P.O. Box 177, Bar Harbor, ME 04609; (207) 288-3338, voice or TDD.

Finding the trailhead: On Mount Desert Island, take Maine Route 3 east

At the summit of Pemetic Mountain. View of Bubble Pond, Cadillac Mountain, and Atlantic Ocean.

HIKE 67 PEMETIC MOUNTAIN

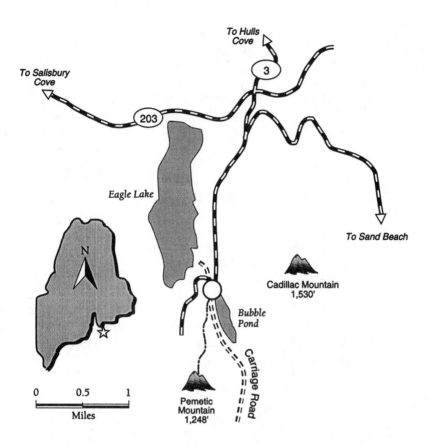

to Hulls Cove. Look for the Park Loop Road and take it south past Eagle Lake to the parking area at Bubble Pond. The parking area is the trailhead.

The hike: Walk to the north end of Bubble Pond at the edge of the parking lot, where a wooden marker indicates the start of the **Pemetic Mountain Trail**. The trail crosses a carriage road and enters woods with spruces, pines, and cedars. The trail is sometimes indistinct, but blue markers attached to trees and blue dabs of paint on rocks indicate the way.

At 0.2 mile, you will walk under a blown-down pine. The trail begins to get steep here and is covered with spruce roots and rocks. At 0.3 mile, the trail bears to the left and becomes very steep as it goes over a granite ledge and boulders. The trail becomes steeper with some scrambling required. At 0.4 mile, you begin to get glimpses of Eagle Lake and the surrounding area. At 0.5 mile, you reach a level spot, with a view of the Atlantic Ocean.

At 0.6 mile, the trail is not as steep as it was, but rocks make walking difficult. You have to pull yourself over a large boulder, but the summit is not far, so take courage. Now you are on the ridge. At 0.7 mile you walk over glacier-scarred ledges to a cairn at the summit. From here you can look down at Bubble Pond. Just across the pond is Cadillac Mountain, and to the north and east, you have unobstructed views of the Atlantic and the Porcupine Islands.

Return to the trailhead by the same route. An alternate hike would be to continue on the carriage road rather than cross over to the Pemetic Mountain Trail. You can walk this gravel path to the end of Bubble Pond and back. This 1.8-mile hike would be suitable for people who use wheelchairs.

HIKE 68 *ACADIA MOUNTAIN*

General description: A hike up a mountain along Somes Sound, the only true fjord in the eastern United States.
General location: South of Somesville between Somes Sound and Echo Lake in the west section of Mount Desert Island, Acadia National Park.
Maps: Maps of Acadia are available at the park entrance and from the USGS; see also the Appalachian Mountain Club map of Mount Desert Island and DeLorme's *The Maine Atlas and Gazetteer*, Map 16.
Degree of difficulty: Moderate.
Length: 2.5 miles round-trip.
Elevations: The summit is 681 feet above sea level.
Water availability: Bring your own water.
Special attractions: Of all the summits in Acadia National Park, only Acadia Mountain has a ridge that runs from east to west. Located on the west shore of Somes Sound, Acadia Mountain offers the best possible view of this striking fjord.
Best season: April through November.
For more information: Superintendent, Acadia National Park, P.O. Box 177, Bar Harbor, ME 04609; (207) 288-3338, voice or TDD.
Finding the trailhead: From Somesville, take Maine Route 102 south to the well-marked Acadia Mountain parking area on the right side of the road. The parking area is the trailhead.

The hike: The trail actually begins across the road from the parking lot. At 0.1 mile from the road, turn left. The trail crosses Man of War Road at 0.2 mile and goes through a mature white pine and spruce forest.

The trail climbs steeply, with switchbacks. Cairns mark the way, as do rock steps. Soon you get a view of Echo Lake. The trail gets easier near the mountaintop. Here is where you get your first partial view of Somes Sound. At 0.6 mile, you reach the west peak of Acadia Mountain. An even better view is yet to come.

HIKE 68 ACADIA MOUNTAIN

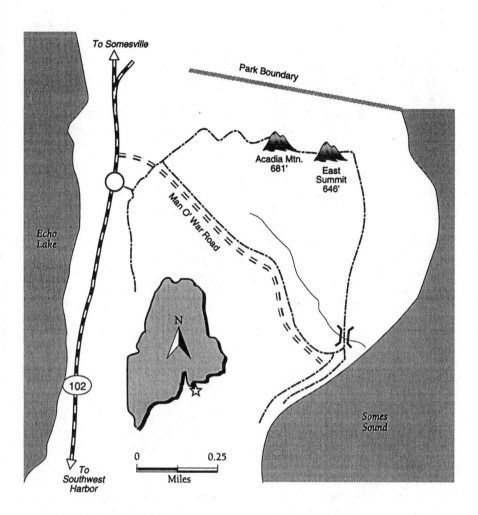

Follow orange markers and cairns to the ridge between the peaks. At 1 mile, you reach the east summit, where you can see all of Somes Sound, the Atlantic Ocean, and other mountains of Acadia. From the east summit, the trail becomes a steep downhill grade. Continue following orange markers and cairns. You may want to stop and check out the view one more time before you get to the bottom.

Soon the trail crosses a bridge over Man of War Brook. The first left turn past the bridge would take you to Somes Sound, but go straight instead until you reach Man of War Road. Follow it back to where you crossed it near the start of your hike. From an old foundation by the side of the road, it is 1 mile back to the trailhead.

HIKE 69 *SHIP HARBOR NATURE TRAIL*

General description: A self-guided tour of a coastal spruce forest, a rocky headland, and a fjordlike harbor.

General location: Ship Harbor on the southwest end of Mount Desert Island, Acadia National Park.

Maps: Check the Eastern National Parks and Monuments Association trail folder, available at the trailhead or at Acadia National Park headquarters in Bar Harbor; see also DeLorme's *The Maine Atlas and Gazetteer*, Map 16.

Length: 1.5-mile loop.

Degree of difficulty: Generally easy, but caution is required where the trail crosses the rocky headland near the mouth of the harbor.

Elevations: No significant elevations encountered.

Water availability: No water available.

Special attractions: This hike is perfect for families with children. The trail folder, available at the trailhead, describes thirteen different aspects of the area's natural history.

Best season: Year-round, but April through November is best, since the trail over the headland can be risky when the rocks are coated with frozen spray.

For more information: Superintendent, Acadia National Park, P.O. Box 177, Bar Harbor, ME 04609; (207) 288-3338.

Finding the trailhead: From the Thompson Island Visitor Center, just past the causeway to Mount Desert Island, take Maine Route 102 south to Southwest Harbor. Just past Southwest Harbor, take a left turn at the junction of ME 102 and ME 102A. Follow ME 102A to a trail sign on the left side of the road, just before the Tremont town line. The parking lot on the left is the trailhead. Begin by the trail sign; a box by the trail contains trail guides.

The hike: Ship Harbor is long, narrow, and lined with rocky bluffs, much like a fjord. The trail begins as a gravel path leading through alders and other pioneer vegetation. This path ends at a fork where you should take the left branch. The trail goes through a spruce forest and past a small bog. Soon, the trail comes to another fork where you can see the actual harbor on your right. Again, go to the left.

The trail now climbs uphill, over exposed spruce roots. At the top of the hill, the trail levels off and passes a plateau covered with low shrubs and stunted spruces. As you walk over the granite ledges here, you get your first glimpse of the open ocean. If you listen carefully, you can hear bells on navigational buoys far out in the channel.

Shortly you will arrive at the mouth of a long, narrow harbor. You can climb around the rocks for a bit and watch fishing boats at work on the ocean. Rangers make it a practice to leave an old lobster trap here so you can examine its workings.

HIKE 69 SHIP HARBOR NATURE TRAIL

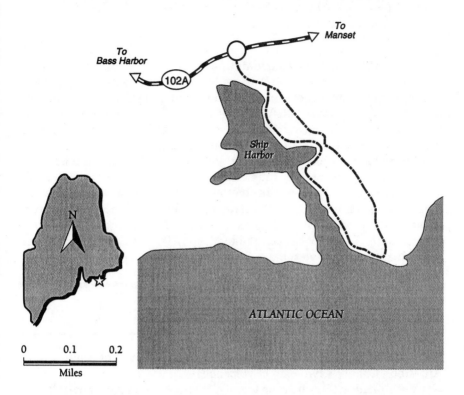

The trail doubles back on itself at the harbor mouth and follows the rocky headland along the protected harbor. Near here in 1739, a ship carrying Irish immigrants was wrecked. The survivors faced the stark realities of a winter on the wild Maine coast. As you walk along the edge of the harbor, you can see sheer granite bluffs on the opposite side. This granite has an orange hue, a perfect subject for color photos.

Heather grows in bunches in the shallow soil. The trail narrows as it climbs the side of the headland. The harbor is on your immediate left, while the steep headland with its jumble of granite boulders and spruces is on your right. At the top of the hill, the trail passes a small wetland then goes down the other side of the hill.

At the bottom of the hill, the trail forks near a small inlet. Here, you can look out at the harbor and a bit of open ocean. A thin strip of salt marsh is gradually building up in this inlet. Take the left fork in the trail and continue on to the head of the harbor.

Near the end of the trail, at marker 13, you overlook the point where a legend tells of an American ship getting stuck in mud here after fleeing from a British warship. This is how Ship Harbor got its name. Continue on the trail back to the parking lot.

AROOSTOOK COUNTY HIKES OVERVIEW

When the bloodless confrontation between the United States and Canada called the "Aroostook War" ended in the early nineteenth century, Aroostook became a separate county in Maine, having previously been included in Penobscot and Washington counties. The boundary lines between Aroostook and surrounding counties are in part a result of work done by the secretary of state at the time, Daniel Webster.

Aroostook is called "The County" by Mainers, since it is the largest in the state. It is, on average, the coldest part of Maine and contains vast woods, streams, and ubiquitous potato fields. It is perhaps the wildest and most underdeveloped part of the state. Aroostook is not home to polluting industries, and land speculators have not yet divided and subdivided its countryside. In such beautiful landscape, its residents retain their individuality and native self-assuredness.

HIKE 70   AROOSTOOK STATE PARK

General description: A hike up a double-peaked mountain, one of Aroostook County's two extinct volcanoes.

General location: South of the town of Presque Isle in Aroostook County.

Maps: A brochure is available at the park entrance or from the Bureau of Parks and Recreation; see also DeLorme's *The Maine Atlas and Gazetteer*, Map 65.

Degree of difficulty: Easy to moderate. Some sections of the hike are quite steep, but otherwise present no difficulty.

Length: 1.5 miles round-trip.

Elevations: South Peak is 1,213 feet above sea level; North Peak is 1,136 feet above sea level.

Water availability: Water is available at the park.

Special attractions: Aroostook State Park is on the shore of Echo Lake, a popular 90-acre body of water that is managed for brook trout. The park features thirty wooded campsites and areas for boat launching, picnicking, and swimming. It also has a number of cross-country ski trails and a network of snowmobile trails. Nearby attractions include the James School, a fully restored one-room schoolhouse, and Haystack Mountain, site of the first successful trans-Atlantic balloon crossing.

Best season: Year-round.

For more information: Aroostook State Park, 87 State Park Road, Presque Isle, ME 04769; (207) 768-8341. Or contact the Bureau of Parks and

Recreation, Maine Department of Conservation, State House Station 22, Augusta, ME 04333, (207) 289-3821.

Finding the trailhead: From points south, take U.S. Highway 1 north to Aroostook County. About 10 miles north of Mars Hill, watch for signs advertising Aroostook State Park. (The park is well-marked from the north as well; take U.S. 1 south from Presque Isle about 5 miles.) The trail to the twin peaks of Quaggy Joe Mountain begins at the state park campground.

The hike: This hike offers good views of the potato fields and woods of Aroostook County. The geologic history of Quaggy Joe's South Peak is of considerable interest. Evidence of an ancient sea can be seen in the mountain's underlying limestone, and an external layer of volcanic matter attests to past volcanic activity.

From the campground, start out on the **South Peak Trail.** The hike is steep and follows a rocky outcropping. Watch for loose stones here. At about 0.4 mile, the trail crosses the state park boundary marked by orange blazes. Be sure not to stray off the trail. At 0.75 mile, you reach the summit.

Go back to the trailhead by the route you just followed. Alternately, you can take the **North-South Peak Trail** to North Peak and go back to the campground by the **North Peak Trail.** The North-South Peak Trail takes you through mixed forest and along a ridge between the peaks. The total added distance is 2.25 miles. North Peak is not as high as South Peak, but offers better views.

HIKE 70 AROOSTOOK STATE PARK

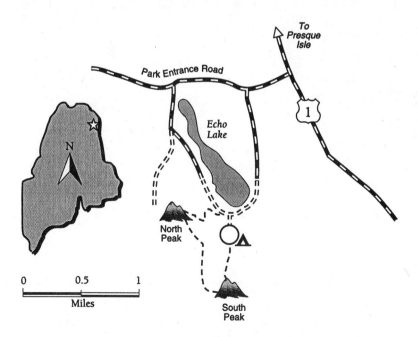

Aroostook State Park.

APPENDIX—A HIKER'S CHECKLIST

Preparing for a hike without using a checklist is much like going grocery shopping without a shopping list: Invariably, you will forget something. The difference between hiking and shopping is that when you are miles down the trail, you cannot simply drive back to the store to get what you need.

The items on this hiker's checklist are only suggestions. You can (and should) tailor your own list to your special needs. Keep in mind that you might encounter adverse conditions and need to be prepared for the worst possible scenario. Also remember that you will not enjoy your hike unless you are comfortable in mind and body.

With that said, here is my suggested list for the equipment you will need while hiking in Maine.

Clothing
____ durable two-piece rain suit
____ nylon wind jacket
____ thermal underwear
____ hat with a visor
____ down-filled vest
____ belt or suspenders
____ several pairs of gloves
____ extra cotton socks
____ extra wool socks
____ comfortable hiking boots
____ shorts for warm weather hikes or swimming
____ bandana
____ wool sweater
____ underwear
____ T-shirts
____ knit cap or balaclava
____ camp moccasins
____ waterproof boots

Food
____ coffee or tea
____ cocoa
____ honey
____ salt and pepper
____ margarine
____ packaged meals
____ powdered soups
____ trail mix
____ jerky
____ dry milk
____ dry herbs and spices
____ garlic bulb
____ bread

Cooking
____ saucepan with cover
____ aluminum foil
____ plastic bowl
____ plastic plate
____ tin or plastic cup
____ knife, fork, and spoon
____ slotted wooden spoon
____ canteen
____ one-gallon collapsible water container
____ water purifiers
____ solar still kit
____ locking food storage bags
____ backpack stove and fuel
____ enameled frying pan
____ stove cleaning accessories
____ copper scouring pad
____ dishrag
____ dishtowel
____ hot pads
____ matches (regular and waterproof)
____ spatula

Fishing
____ rods
____ reels
____ leaders
____ lures
____ flies
____ forceps
____ assorted split shot
____ assorted hooks

Fishing (cont.)
____ nail clippers
____ fishing license and regulations
____ pocket tape
____ lip balm (for use as fly
     floatant)
____ diamond honer for hooks

Photography
____ camera
____ film and canisters
____ extra lenses
____ filters
____ extra film
____ lens brush or tissue
____ flash attachment
____ monopod or tripod

Miscellaneous
____ sleeping bag, pad, and tent
     (for overnight stays)
____ waterproof match case
____ prescription medication
____ moleskin pads
____ extra insoles
____ wild food guide
____ pen and paper
____ walking stick
____ pliers
____ aspirin

Miscellaneous (cont.)
____ waterproof tape
____ gauze
____ liniment or witch hazel
____ sunscreen
____ safety pins
____ small sewing kit
____ sunglasses
____ whistle
____ salt tablets
____ toothpaste and toothbrush
____ dental floss
____ baking soda
____ toothpicks
____ mirror
____ hiking guide
____ insect repellent
____ folding candle lantern
____ candles
____ toilet paper
____ space blanket
____ binoculars
____ your favorite book
____ safety pins
____ compass
____ area maps
____ knapsack
____ pack basket
____ crystal-controlled weather
     radio

ABOUT THE AUTHOR

Tom Seymour began his writing career as a correspondent for the *Bangor Daily News* in 1975. Specializing in articles about hunting, fishing, nature, and edible wild plants, Seymour is now a regular columnist for both Belfast's *Republican Journal*, Maine's weekly newspaper, *The Maritime Sportsman*, a Canadian publication, and the *Maine Sportsman*, New England's largest outdoor publication.

Seymour's freelance credits include articles in the *Maine Issue, Sun-Day, Backwoodsman Magazine, Young American, Popular Lures, Fur-Fish-Game, Muzzle Blasts, Bangor Daily News*, and *New England Game and Fish*. He also writes an annual hunting supplement for the *Republican Journal*, and one of his columns for that newspaper won a New England Press Association Excellence in Journalism Award in 1987.

When not writing or participating in outdoor activities, Seymour plays the Great Highland bagpipes. He was editor of the *Pine Tree Highlander*, a quarterly newsletter devoted to Scottish culture. Seymour is also a regularly featured guest on *The Maine Outdoorsman* television show, a popular Maine outdoor-oriented program.

OUT HERE THERE'S NO ONE TO ASK DIRECTION

Let Falcon Be Your Guide

The **FALCON**GUIDES series consists of recreational guidebooks designed to help you safely enjoy the great outdoors. Each 6 x 9" softcover book features up-to-date maps, photos, and detailed information on access, hazards, side trip special attractions, and more. So whether you're planning you first adventure have enjoyed the outdoors for years, a **FALCON**GUIDE makes an ideal companio

For more information about these and other Falcon Press books, please visit your local bookstore, or call or write for a free catalog.

FALCO

HIKING NOTES

HIKING NOTES

HIKING NOTES

HIKING NOTES